"THE PRIME MOVER"

CHARLES L. HUTCHINSON AND THE MAKING OF
THE ART INSTITUTE OF CHICAGO

Executive Director of Publications: Robert V. Sharp; Editor of *Museum Studies*: Gregory Nosan; Guest Editor: Amy R. Peltz; Designer: Salvador Cruz, Jr.; Production: Carolyn Ziebarth and Kate Kotan; Photo Editor: Joseph Mohan; Subscription and Circulation: Bryan D. Miller and Molly Heyen.

This publication was typeset in Topaz and Stempel Garamond. Color separations and printing by Meridian Printing, East Greenwich, Rhode Island.

This publication is volume 36, number 1 of *Museum Studies*, which is published semiannually by the Art Institute of Chicago Publications Department, 111 South Michigan Avenue, Chicago, Illinois, 60603-6404.

For information on subscriptions and back issues, consult www.artic.edu/aic/books/msbooks or contact (312) 443-3786 or pubsmus@artic.edu.

Ongoing support for *Museum Studies* has been provided by a grant for scholarly catalogues and publications from the Andrew W. Mellon Foundation.

This book was produced using paper certified by the Forest Stewardship Council.
ISSN 0069-3235
ISBN 978-0-86559-238-4

Unless otherwise noted, all illustrations are from photographs or other works in the collections of the Department of Archives, the Art Institute of Chicago, and were photographed by the Department of Imaging © The Art Institute of Chicago. All works of art in the Art Institute's collection were also photographed by the Department of Imaging © The Art Institute of Chicago. Some images in this publication are subject to copyright and may not be reproduced without the approval of the rights holder. Every effort has been made to contact copyright holders for all reproductions.

Sources of quotations in figure captions: p. 9, fig. 1: "Critics of Chicago Pronounced Unfair; Good Works Listed," 1910, unidentified newspaper clipping, scrapbook of clippings, box 3, Charles L. Hutchinson Collection, Newberry Library, Chicago; p. 14, fig. 8: Thomas Wakefield Goodspeed, "Charles Lawrence Hutchinson," in *The University of Chicago Biographical Sketches*, vol. 2 (University of Chicago Press, 1925), p. 28; p. 17, fig. 10: Hamlin Garland, "A Citizen of Chicago," *New York Times*, Oct. 19, 1924, p. X14; p. 17, fig. 11: Frances Kinsley Hutchinson to Frances Glessner, Nov. 7, 1910, Frances Macbeth Glessner and John J. Glessner Journals (1879–1921), Chicago History Museum; p. 21, fig. 4: William M. R. French to M. D. Follansbee, Dec. 17, 1909, French Papers, Art Institute of Chicago Archives (hereafter cited as AIC Archives); p. 41, fig. 8: French to Henry Reinhardt, Aug. 31, 1908, French Papers; p. 50, fig. 5: French to John T. McCutcheon, Feb. 8, 1909, French Papers; p. 60, fig. 16: William Rainey Harper to Charles L. Hutchinson, Dec. 23, 1905, William Rainey Harper Papers, box 8, folder 13, Special Collections Research Center, University of Chicago Library; p. 62, fig. 19: French to Harrison S. Morris, Jan. 8, 1906, French Papers; p. 72, fig. 4: French to Sara Hallowell, Mar. 18, 1912, French Papers; p. 74, fig. 7: French to Frederic C. Bartlett, Sept. 13, 1907; p. 85, fig. 8: Bertha E. Jaques to Frances Kinsley Hutchinson, Oct. 11, 1924, memorial scrapbook, box 1, Hutchinson Papers, AIC Archives.

FRONT COVER: Charles L. Hutchinson (right), his wife Frances, and Martin A. Ryerson in Pompeii, c. 1904.

BACK COVER: (clockwise from top right) Detail of a vintage postcard showing the Art Institute with famous early aviator Walter Brookins flying overhead, c. 1911 (Collection of Celia Hilliard); Hutchinson at Wychwood, c. 1920 (p. 78, fig. 1, detail); Central stair and hall of the Art Institute's first custom-built structure on Michigan Avenue (p. 18, fig. 1, detail); The Hutchinsons with Martin and Carrie Ryerson in Sri Lanka, winter 1896 (p. 46, fig. 1, detail).

OPPOSITE: The Art Institute under construction, c. 1892 (p. 33, fig. 19, detail).

ART
INSTITVTE
CHICAGO

THE ART INSTITUTE OF CHICAGO
MUSEUM STUDIES

"THE PRIME MOVER"

CHARLES L. HUTCHINSON AND THE MAKING OF
THE ART INSTITUTE OF CHICAGO

CELIA HILLARD

FOREWORD

CHARLES L. HUTCHINSON is arguably the single most important individual to have shaped the direction and fortunes of the Art Institute of Chicago. President of the museum's board of trustees from 1882 until his death in 1924, he took direct responsibility for almost every aspect of its administrative and curatorial programs. Early in his tenure, he was described by his colleague William M. R. French, the first director of the Art Institute, as "the prime mover in everything here." Decades later, the second director, Robert Harshe, put it slightly differently: "He was the Art Institute and it will stand as his most permanent monument."

Hutchinson embodied the Chicago spirit. Energetic and open minded, he was as committed to philanthropy and civic affairs as he was successful in business. He succeeded his father in a number of enterprises, particularly the Corn Exchange Bank, and held a seat on the Board of Trade. He was also a trustee of the University of Chicago, the Chicago Symphony Orchestra, and Hull House; a guarantor of the World's Columbian Exposition and head of its Fine Arts Department; and a long-standing member of the prestigious Commercial Club, in which capacity he staunchly supported Daniel Burnham's Plan of Chicago, which exerted a substantial influence on the city's subsequent development.

It is thus surprising that, until now, Hutchinson has not been the subject of a substantial study. More attention has been paid to his friend and fellow trustee Martin A. Ryerson, who built a large and important collection and gave it to

Detail of William M. R. French's travel diary for April 4, 1889. French and Charles L. Hutchinson visited numerous cultural institutions across Europe seeking ideas for the design of the Art Institute's own galleries. This sketch depicts a staircase in the Lateran Museum, Rome, that may have inspired the Grand Staircase in the Art Institute's 1893 Allerton Building.

the museum. For this he will forever be remembered. But Hutchinson can truly be said to have *built* the museum. Although he, too, collected and donated works of art, he was more of a "bricks and mortar man," securing the site on the lakefront and commissioning the design of the grand new Michigan Avenue building. During his tenure this structure was enlarged to include Gunsaulus Hall, McKinlock Court, and an Old Masters gallery that was named in his honor.

Whether building the museum's collection or its physical plant, Hutchinson also looked beyond Chicago. He was influenced deeply by his many travels, during which he acquired not only objects for the Art Institute but also ideas about what it could and should be. As shown by the cover image of this issue—a 1909 photograph of Hutchinson with his wife, Frances, and Ryerson, all consulting guidebooks in the ruins of Pompeii—he looked to Europe's rich visual, intellectual, and civic culture as a model. During such trips, he formed a conviction that the young city of Chicago and its inhabitants would benefit from experiencing great art and architecture, and a determination to help them do so.

Perhaps Hutchinson's greatest legacy is that he instilled in the museum a strong commitment to the life of the city. As he once said, "Art is not destined for a small and privileged class. Art is democratic, it is of the people, and for the people." We are grateful to Celia Hilliard for telling the story of Hutchinson's many contributions to the Art Institute. This book, with its elegant text and illuminating illustrations, will prove a lasting addition to the history of the museum and the cultural life of Chicago.

JAMES CUNO
President and Eloise W. Martin Director

ACKNOWLEDGMENTS

THE LAST DECADES of the nineteenth century witnessed the birth and phenomenal rise of the public art museum, first on the East Coast and, subsequently, all across America. In just one city, however, did a single individual preside for more than forty years over the development of its primary arts organization. Charles L. Hutchinson reigned as president of the Art Institute of Chicago from 1882 until his death in 1924. This extraordinary accomplishment prompted my curiosity, encouraging me to investigate how his character, perspective, and leadership style shaped the museum during its formative years. As I discovered, Hutchinson was the ultimate public citizen, an important voice in the founding of not only the Art Institute but many other enduring civic and cultural entities. Examining his life required that I research across a wide range of subjects, drawing on a broad selection of archival and other resources.

My inquiry began with Helen Lefkowitz Horowitz's classic study *Culture and the City: Cultural Philanthropy in Chicago from the 1880s to 1917*, still the essential starting point for any investigation of this topic. William Cronon's fine history *Nature's Metropolis: Chicago and the Great West*, was crucial to my understanding of the growth of Chicago commerce in the second half of the nineteenth century. Also of much interest were unpublished dissertations by Anne Felicia Cierpik, Aileen Hollis, and Vera L. Zolberg (available in the Art Institute's Ryerson and Burnham Libraries). Writings by Art Institute curator Martha Wolff and University of Chicago professor emeritus Neil Harris were useful in analyzing the taste and acquisitions of Hutchinson's friend and fellow trustee, Martin A. Ryerson.

Among the many archives I turned to, the Art Institute's were indispensable. They comprise a particularly abundant source of information about Hutchinson and his milieu, and I offer warm thanks to archivist Bart Ryckbosch for guiding me through its extensive and unique holdings. Bart's encyclopedic knowledge, invaluable suggestions, and generous spirit enlivened this inquiry from start to finish. His associates Danielle N. Kramer and Deborah Webb offered friendly assistance. Bart, Danielle, and Debbie also helped locate one-of-a-kind images to bring the story to life, and facilitate their publication, enabling many items to be seen by the public for the first time. Jack Brown, executive director of the Ryerson and Burnham Libraries, helped orient the path of my research. His colleagues Susan Augustine and Mary Woolever called my attention to useful resources.

Documents that shed light on Hutchinson's life reside in the archives of several other Chicago institutions, and I extend heartfelt thanks to their staffs for the aid they offered. For their generous assistance I would especially like to acknowledge Lesley Martin, Robert Medina, and Deborah Vaughan of the Chicago History Museum; Martha Briggs, Diane Dillon, and Paul Gehl of the Newberry Library; Dan Meyer and Alice Schreyer of the Special Collections Research Center of the University of Chicago Library; and the staff of the Special Collections and Preservation Division of the Chicago Public Library. Not only did these individuals assist me while I researched the project, but they also shared the exceptional archival images in their care, often arranging for the photography of those that had not yet been shot.

Elsewhere, I am grateful for the cordial help of John Smith and his colleagues at the Archives of American Art, Washington, D. C. I owe special thanks to Mary Daniels of the Frances Loeb Library at the Graduate School of Design, Harvard University, and also to the staff of the Historical

Collections at the Baker Library of Harvard Business School. Robert C. Hellebusch, Pelee Club historian, generously provided early photographs of this rustic retreat.

I am also indebted to several individuals who offered advice and shared the fruits of their own research, including Art Institute trustee Karen B. Alexander, who recounted the history of the ancient art collection in an earlier issue of *Museum Studies*; distinguished decorative arts historian Sharon S. Darling; former School of the Art Institute president Anthony Jones, whose forthcoming history of the School of the Art Institute will add much to the story of the organization's development; independent scholar John K. Notz, Jr., who has written extensively on Lake Geneva properties, including the Hutchinson estate; and William Tyre, executive director and curator of the Glessner House Museum.

Numerous curators at the Art Institute graciously contributed their expertise. I thank Judith A. Barter, Sarah E. Kelly, Denise Mahoney, and Brandon K. Ruud, all of the Department of American Art; Karen Manchester, Mary Greuel, and Janice Katz in the Department of Asian and Ancient Art; Martha Wolff and Adrienne Jeske in the Department of Medieval through Modern European Painting and Sculpture; and Barbara Hinde and Mark Pascale in the Department of Prints and Drawings. I am appreciative as well of the scholarly encouragement of president and director James Cuno.

The members of other museum departments at the museum also made this project possible in diverse ways. I am deeply indebted to my collaborators in the Department of Publications, under the able direction of Robert V. Sharp. The concept of this work was first discussed many months ago with Susan F. Rossen and *Museum Studies* editor Greg Nosan, whose judgment and imagination helped to focus this investigation. The final product owes much to the splendid guidance of editor Amy R. Peltz, whose suggestions, refinements, and patience were unfailing. Carolyn Ziebarth expertly managed the production process, and Kate Kotan ensured that every illustration looked as handsome as possible on the page. Photo editor Joseph Mohan tirelessly tracked down hard-to-find images and worked with staff at the Art Institute and elsewhere to create publishable versions of these items. Department assistant Molly Heyen offered vital help at various junctures of the project. Nancy Behall, Clare Britt, Christopher Gallagher, Robert Hashimoto, Robert Lifson, Caroline Nutley, and Amy Zavaleta, all of the Department of Imaging, created beautiful photographs of works of art and archival items in the Art Institute's collections. I am also grateful to Salvador Cruz of the Graphics Department, who created a design with just the right balance between old and new. Danny Frank of Meridian Printing saw the issue through color separation, printing, and binding with utmost care.

Finally, I add loving thanks to my husband, David. I have relied throughout on his extensive knowledge of the Art Institute's collections and their donors. He is first, last, and always, a devoted student of the museum and a constant advocate of its best interests. This issue is dedicated to him and to all the avid readers who have explored the abundant resources of the Art Institute through many notable volumes of *Museum Studies*.

CELIA HILLIARD

"THE ORIGINAL ART IMPULSE"

THE CITY OF CHICAGO, still sparsely settled at the time of its incorporation in 1837, grew fast and raw (FIG. 1). Its boundless commercial promise drew men of unusual vigor: shrewd, forceful, and determined to elbow their way to the top. Whatever their chosen commodity—farm machinery, grain, lumber, pork, or railroads—they succeeded beyond all expectation, achieving economic control over wide stretches of the surrounding region's rich natural resources, amassing large fortunes in the process. Unsurprisingly, their driving ambition gave rise to much that was coarse, pompous, and mean, and that pushed to the side defenders of the simpler virtues and advocates for the development of a broad civic culture.

In the course of time, however, these others found their champions, and foremost among them must stand Charles L. Hutchinson. Often called the city's "First Citizen," his greatest accomplishment was the establishment of the Art Institute of Chicago, an enterprise arguably more enduring than those mighty fiefdoms built on grain and pork.[1] He assumed the presidency of the board of trustees in 1882, when he was just twenty-eight years old and the museum hardly more than a hopeful aspiration in the minds of a few Chicagoans. He held the office to the end of his life. His unwavering aim was to lay the foundations for a great institution, nurture its growth, and ensure its stability. Hutchinson's manner was humble, his tastes catholic. For forty years his was the most important opinion. His death on October 7, 1924, was declared a public calamity.[2]

Yet today Hutchinson is perhaps the least remembered of the museum's founding generation. Clarence Buckingham, Charles W. Fullerton, and Frank W. Gunsaulus are names that resonate. Among the twenty-five distinguished citizens memorialized in Pioneer Court, a small plaza on Michigan Avenue at the Chicago River, it is Martin A. Ryerson who represents the Art Institute. Hutchinson's grave at Graceland Cemetery is marked with a small stone, flat to the ground, almost invisible from the road. His true monument is the Art Institute itself, and his story, so closely intertwined with the museum's evolution, bears retelling.

* * *

When Hutchinson became president of the fledgling Art Institute, just three American cities, all in the East—Boston, New York, and Philadelphia—boasted major art museums. By the time of his death, not only was the Art Institute poised on the edge of international recognition, but significant organizations devoted to the display of art had also sprung up across the United States, including in other midwestern cities such as Cincinnati, Cleveland, Milwaukee, Minneapolis, St. Louis, and Toledo. This swift growth was part of the tide of cultural philanthropy that swept across late-nineteenth- and early-twentieth-century America, initiated primarily by individuals like Hutchinson—cultured, native-born sons of the great Gilded Age magnates.[3] During this younger generation's childhood, the cities their families called home were also in their infancy, dominated by commercial concerns and lacking the amenities already common in the metropolises of the East. Thanks to their wealth, these men traveled widely in the United States and, above all, Europe, where they were

FIGURE 1. Michigan Avenue and Randolph Street, before 1871. Hutchinson observed in an October 1910 debate at the Chicago Woman's Club that the city had grown from a town to a metropolis in just one generation, so "it is not strange that we should present to the chance visitor many things that appear crude and provincial."

9

FIGURE 2. Crosby's Opera House, located on Washington Street between State and Dearborn streets, was constructed in 1865, financed by a lottery whose prize was the building itself. The fourth floor hosted artists' studios, and its long skylit gallery provided the perfect environment for their work. Undoubtedly one of the architectural gems of the city, it was destroyed in 1871 by the Great Chicago Fire. Chicago History Museum, ICHi–01727. Lithograph by James W. Sheahan, published by Jevni and Almini.

for commercial excess, in the mid-nineteenth century it already enjoyed a burgeoning artistic and philanthropic life. Even among the early settlers there were individuals with an appetite for books, learning, and the fine arts. They organized readings and concerts, saw the great actors of the day in new theaters downtown, and after Crosby's Opera House was finished in 1865, listened to famous singers performing in the grand style (FIG. 2). Moreover, as the prosperous elite built mansions along the lakefront (FIG. 3), they—like their peers on the East Coast, where there were also still few public museums—often made room for private art galleries, which suggested close acquaintance with elevated thoughts and ideas. As a youth, Charles Hutchinson felt at home in this refined milieu. It was open only to the elite, however, and would clearly require leaders of energy and vision to open it to the whole city and realize its full potential. Luckily, this nascent cosmopolitanism itself equipped Hutchinson with the skills and commitment needed to make this world of culture available to all.

The paintings in the city's first recorded public art exhibition, held in 1859 in Burch's Building at the corner of Wabash Avenue and Lake Street, were drawn primarily from these local collections.[4] Some of the canvases were frank copies of great works or modestly attributed ("after Raphael" or "supposed Sir Joshua Reynolds"), but others were boldly credited to Bruegel, Titian, and even Da Vinci. However dubious these labels appear in retrospect, the essential point is not the authenticity of the works themselves so much as what they represented: the desire to create a more cultured society to complement the city's explosive commercial and physical growth.

This first exhibition, and others that followed, were all temporary. Most of the pictures on display had been purchased back East or abroad, and the focus was mainly on European artists, although the work of notable American painters such as Albert Bierstadt, Jasper Cropsey, and John Frederick Kensett was also in evidence. A local community of artists coalesced slowly, proceeding from the success of

exposed to grand cultural institutions that their fathers could not have imagined; they returned to their hometowns eager to "civilize" them. Coming of age at a critical juncture in the lives of their cities, they were able to help shape these places according to their ideals, founding libraries, museums, and symphonies—organizations intended to make the elevating forces of culture available to all. Thanks to their enthusiasm, generosity, and social connections, their success was unprecedented. Hutchinson, the son of a meat packer and speculator, stood at the helm of the Midwest's preeminent museum for over forty years, and epitomizes these changes. Like his peers, he was a product of his time and place and, simultaneously, exactly what it needed. Through his life we can trace the development not only of the Art Institute, but of trends that transformed the American cultural landscape.

* * *

Although today the Art Institute's origins are closely identified with its 1893 Beaux Arts structure on Michigan Avenue (the present Allerton Building), the museum did not emerge from a cultural vacuum. Despite Chicago's early reputation its two most prominent members, the portrait painter G. P. A. Healy and the sculptor Leonard Volk. Artists formed various associations, with some taking studios in Crosby's Opera House, where a long skylit gallery on the fourth floor served as a handsome showcase for their works. The most important of these groups was the Chicago Academy of Design, formally organized in 1866 and supported by dues (FIG. 4). It was patterned on New York's National Academy of Design, conducting classes and staging exhibitions, but its larger purpose was to stimulate public interest in the arts and promote the careers of its members. The group assembled a small collection of paintings and casts, and eventually built an imposing structure housing large galleries, classrooms, and lecture halls, but all of this burned to the ground in the Great Chicago Fire of 1871. The loss was so devastating that many artists chose simply to leave the city. After a time the remnants of the academy made efforts to regroup. Although they acquired space in the well-situated Pike's Building at the southwest corner of Monroe and State streets and resumed holding classes and shows, the organization never regained its momentum. Due to bungled efforts and periods of economic depression, the number of full-time pupils dwindled and large debts accrued, exacerbating internal tensions.

In December 1877, over the objections of a faction that believed in strict control by professional artists, the academy voted to enlist the help of some public-spirited businessmen. The bylaws were rewritten to provide for the election of fifteen trustees to administer the enterprise's affairs. It was hoped that they would fund some of its operations as well. In short order, the new trustees discovered that the academy's resources had been exaggerated and its debts understated. These were probably not insurmountable obstacles, but the businessmen were frustrated by the artists' hostility to their involvement in any matter except financial support. The trustees concluded that even sturdy management could not place the group on a strong foundation and declared there was "no sense paying for dead horses."[5] In the spring of 1879, they resigned in a body, leaving the artists to flounder in the face of their creditors.

FIGURE 3. Terrace Row, on Michigan Avenue between Van Buren and Congress streets, was an elite residential enclave built in 1856. Consisting of eleven attached houses faced in marble, it burned completely in the Great Chicago Fire. Chicago History Museum, ICHi-04427.

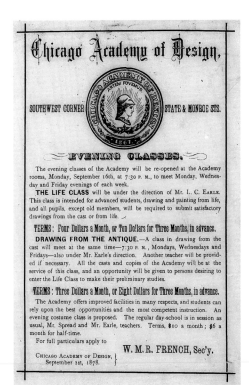

FIGURE 4. Advertisement for evening classes at the Chicago Academy of Design, the earliest forerunner of the Art Institute. It was founded in 1866, when the only comparable organizations in the United States were in New York and Philadelphia. William French served as the secretary of this group as well as of its successor, the Chicago Academy of Fine Arts.

Although the businessmen withdrew from the academy, they did not abandon the idea of an institution to encourage the fine arts in Chicago. In May 1879, a few of them sent a letter to other citizens they presumed to share their interest in forming a new association. Among the twenty men who attended an exploratory meeting at the Palmer House Hotel were former academy trustees and a handful of the city's power brokers. Also present was the twenty-five-year-old banker Hutchinson, the youngest man in the room.

Enthusiasm was high and steps were immediately taken to organize what would become the Chicago Academy of Fine Arts. Three classes of membership were established. Governing members had voting privileges. Annual members would enjoy free admission to the anticipated exhibitions and receptions. Honorary members were drawn from the ranks of local artists or patrons of the arts, or individuals who rendered "eminent services" to the association. In what was either a prudent move or a cynical coup, the trustees

acquired at a modest cost all of the artwork, fixtures, and furniture that once belonged to the old Academy of Design, which had been seized by the court after the group defaulted on its obligations.[6]

Other continuities existed between the two organizations. The new Academy of Fine Arts leased the Academy of Design's old rooms, retained a few of its longtime teachers, and offered a similar curriculum. William M. R. French, secretary of the old group, was named administrative head of the new organization, with the same title. The school was not closed for a single day, and the majority of its classes continued. There was no mistaking, however, that the scope and aims of the academy were broader than those of any previous organization and that its priorities had shifted: the trustees agreed that all monies from governing members and any other large donations would be reserved for creating a museum.

The first board of trustees was dominated by men from the Board of Trade, which regulated grain commerce, with

FIGURE 5. Hutchinson as a young boy, in a daguerreotype taken a few years after his family moved to Chicago from Milwaukee, where his father—a native New Englander—had settled to learn the grain trade. Chicago History Museum, ICHi-61820.

some merchants and bankers in the mix. The group included a few serious collectors. Its first president, George Armour, owned several large grain elevators along the Chicago River. He served for one year and was succeeded by Levi Leiter, a merchant and real estate investor who had recently withdrawn from a lucrative partnership with Marshall Field. Several other trustees were attentive to the institution's affairs, yet for men who had professed a strong commitment, some were unexpectedly lax in performing their duties. They typically arrived late to meetings, and a year after incorporation a number had still not even paid their governing member fees. The organization was in fact running a deficit, and instead of moving to more spacious quarters as planned, it was forced to lease the same modest rooms again. No substantial gifts had been received, nor had any new patrons appeared. As French recalled some years later, "It was believed that Mr. Armour was ready to give a considerable sum to the new institution, but he waited for Mr. Leiter to cooperate with him."[7] To general astonishment, neither man did more than help defray some ordinary bills. Armour tried to persuade Field, one of the five signers of the petition to incorporate, to support the fledgling enterprise and even to officiate as its next president, but was turned down.

Only one man—Hutchinson—had labored consistently to set the Academy of Fine Arts on a sturdy foundation. Part of a small committee charged with managing the group's practical affairs, he became indispensable to every major and minor project. After he was named vice president in 1881, he and Albert Hayden, another early trustee, personally raised sufficient money to carry the art school forward and advance plans for a permanent location. While there were half-hearted efforts to replace Leiter with another prominent figurehead, Leiter himself was said to have declared that Hutchinson could "do more for the institution than all the rest put together."[8] Certainly no one intimately connected with the group was at all surprised when Hutchinson was elected president of the board the following year. That same day he reported on property for sale at the southwest corner of Michigan Avenue and Van Buren Street. He announced that he had already secured almost two-thirds of the financing needed to buy the lot and build, and asked the trustees as a group to raise the balance. He also proposed

FIGURE 6. Benjamin P. Hutchinson, shown on the cover of *Harper's Weekly*, May 10, 1890, at the height of his fame. His dramatic rise and fall was later recounted in Edward Jerome Dies's *The Plunger: A Tale of the Wheat Pit* (1929). Chicago History Museum, ICHi-61819.

that the organization change its name, although it was not until a formal and unanimous vote of the governing members that the new title was officially adopted: the Art Institute of Chicago.

* * *

Charles Lawrence Hutchinson's rapid rise and long tenure at the helm of what would become Chicago's premier cultural institution can be at least partially traced to his unusual family circumstances and atypical youth. He was born March 7, 1854, in Lynn, Massachusetts, where his father, Benjamin P. Hutchinson, had begun a career in that city's burgeoning shoe industry (FIG. 6). Eyeing the more lucrative commodities business, he moved his young family west, settling first in Milwaukee to learn the grain trade. When Hutchinson had mastered the fundamentals, he moved to

Chicago, where he may have paid no more than $5 for his seat on the Board of Trade. He made a fortune packing meat during the Civil War, and his firm was the first to move to the Union Stockyards when they opened in 1866.[9] Hailed as a "deep, sagacious operator," Hutchinson also speculated heavily in grain, garnering enormous profits.[10] In 1870 he founded the Corn Exchange National Bank to make loans to members of the Board of Trade dealing in grain and provisions. Flush with surplus cash, he invested in carpeting, coffee, downtown real estate, furniture, insurance, tea, and even whiskey and California wines—anything he could buy cheap and sell for more. His signature was deemed "gilt-edge . . . good for any contract he may make." In all these ventures, whether alone or with partners, he was identified as "the main man" and "the ruling spirit." Although it is likely that he himself could never give an exact account of his assets, at the height of his legendary career he was worth millions.

As Hutchinson's elder son, Charles grew up amid all the privileges of the city's new aristocracy (FIG. 5). His mother, Sarah Ingalls, was in fact from old Yankee stock, a direct descendant of the family that had settled the town of Lynn in 1629. He had three sisters, Kate, Helen, and Hattie (this last did not survive to adulthood), and a brother, William, younger than Charles by seventeen years. The family occupied a series of fine townhouses on South Wabash Avenue and East Harrison Street, with summertime visits to the Hyde Park House (FIG. 7). Situated in a beautiful grove at 53rd Street and the lakefront, this South Side resort had easy access to the beach and hosted weekly dance hops, band concerts, and moonlight picnics on its wide verandas. Here the Hutchinsons mingled with the families of other prominent Chicagoans like Potter Palmer, S. D. Kimbark, George Farnsworth, and W. W. Kimball. Charles was remembered as good-humored, bright, and affectionate (FIG. 8). While his sisters attended the all-girls Dearborn Seminary, he was enrolled in the Chicago High School, an eminent coeducational institution with distinguished faculty. Its principal, George Howland, a graduate of Amherst College, was a Classics scholar who published translations of Virgil and Homer, had written a widely used English grammar, and composed poetry in his leisure time. He was described as "a Puritan without bigotry," devoted to the public schools of

FIGURE 7. Hyde Park House, a resort at 53rd Street and Lake Michigan, where the Hutchinson family spent summer vacations among other members of Chicago's elite.

FIGURE 8. Instructional map of New England, drawn, colored, and signed by "Charley Hutchinson" in elementary school. Later a high school classmate described him as "an almost perfect student." Charles L. Hutchinson Papers, The Newberry Library, Chicago.

America and the development of their pupils as reflective, independent thinkers.[11] Bookish and ambitious, Charles revered Howland. He was himself a favorite of Anne Trimmingham, assistant to the principal and teacher of drawing, who encouraged his budding interest in art. Charles made occasional visits to the galleries in Crosby's Opera House, and it was also during these years that he first encountered William French, whom he would later appoint director of the new Art Institute. In the early 1870s, French was holding art classes in his rented rooms on Wabash Avenue. Charles and his friends would drop in to paint or draw from a plaster statue of femme fatale Elsie Venner, the title character of Oliver Wendell Holmes's popular novel *Elsie Venner: A Romance of Destiny* (1861). Years later, Hutchinson's friend Calvin Cobb reminded him, "You did have her snakeship in marble, which you should treasure as the original art impulse," suggesting that this alluring sculpture had been the germ of his lifelong attraction to art.[12]

An equally important influence was his family's membership in St. Paul's Universalist Church, a liberal congregation where strict adherence to doctrine was deemphasized in favor of broad humanitarian ideals. These were the years when the celebrated minister William Henry Ryder occupied the pulpit. He was one of a group of charismatic and learned clergymen, sometimes called "the God talkers," who held considerable sway over Chicago society.[13] Their sermons exhorting the rich to a life of charity and public service were reprinted in the Monday papers, and their words had the power to open the purses of the most miserly tycoons. Charles attended St. Paul's Sunday school from age six and over the years absorbed its message of selfless devotion to one's fellow humans more earnestly than most. By age fourteen, he had already assembled his first major donation: $100, which he collected by selling dime tickets for a fair to benefit the Newsboys and Bootblacks' Home, a South Side charity that provided homeless youth lodging and supper while they searched for work (FIG. 9).

Valedictorian of his high school class, Hutchinson wished to continue his education at a prestigious university.[14] His father, however, had other ideas, and thus the young man spent a year in the grain business and a year in the packinghouse, starting as a clerk earning just $3 a week. On his twenty-first

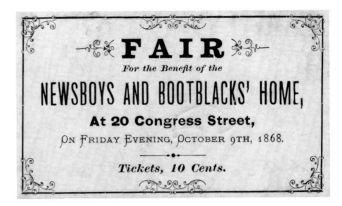

FIGURE 9. Hutchinson organized his first charitable endeavor at age fourteen, selling tickets to a benefit fair for homeless young bootblacks and newsboys. He contributed his own money and solicited funds from his mother, sisters, and friends. The endeavor must have been particularly meaningful to him, as he saved a ticket among his papers his entire life. Charles L. Hutchinson Papers, The Newberry Library, Chicago.

birthday, his father made him a present of $25,000, some of which he used to speculate in the markets, with disastrous results. Thereafter Charles entered the Corn Exchange Bank, where the work and atmosphere were a far better match for his temperament. He advanced through every department until he was named assistant cashier, and in 1880 he acquired a one-fourth interest in the bank.[15] Not many years later, in 1886, he succeeded to its presidency.

Although his background was privileged, Hutchinson was far from a typical second-generation Chicago prince. With his advantages came immense responsibilities, for his father was by no means a typical patriarch. He was seldom home, but rather stayed in downtown hotels or slept in his office or his "Century Club," which consisted of a few rented rooms and a kitchen in the Rialto Building on Van Buren Street, directly behind the Board of Trade.[16] All tasks relating to his family's domestic life were therefore assigned to the barely adolescent Charles.[17] The boy was charged with keeping the household accounts, paying wages and bills, deciding on purchases, organizing trips, and even approving his sisters' suitors. In the evenings, he presided at the head of the table, while his father, who loved to cook and possessed a butcher's knowledge of meat, was likely down at the Century, frying chops and swapping stories with a handful of clerks and reporters who adored his irascible vitality. Or possibly "Old Hutch" was off at a music hall, where he liked to sit next to the bass drummer and stay for hours, doubled up in laughter at the world's oldest vaudeville jokes.[18] The elder Hutchinson was utterly indifferent to social opinion. He never adopted the trappings of his hard-won success and appeared to most people like a man who would be most comfortable behind the counter of a country store, wearing the same high collar, faded tailcoat, and doeskin pants that were already out of fashion thirty years before.[19] His true home remained the trading floor, where he moved with perfect pitch, always alone, unpredictable, a terror to men of lesser talent. He was a strangely compelling figure, and it cannot have been easy to survive and develop in his wake.

Many sons (and daughters) of "the old roosters," as the kingpins of commerce were sometimes dubbed, escaped to entirely other realms and found success as artists, diplomats, gentlemen farmers, politicians, publishers, or avid travelers or collectors—anything but stewards of the industries that handily supported them in style for the rest of their lives. The tycoons, however they may have longed for heirs to carry on the family businesses, were with few exceptions staunch patriarchs, secure at the head of conventional households and often proud of providing their children freedom and the advantages they themselves had never enjoyed. Samuel Allerton, a founder of the Union Stock Yards and father of Robert (who would eventually become one of the museum's greatest benefactors), remarked with pleased amazement to his friend Adolphus Clay Bartlett, the hardware magnate (whose son Frederic would one day present the museum with Georges Seurat's *A Sunday on La Grande Jatte—1884*), "Just think, Bartlett, of our having art boys for sons!"[20]

Young "Charley," shouldering responsibilities beyond his years, was the biblical good son (FIG. 10). Steady, conscientious, deeply attached to his mother and siblings, he did everything that was asked of him. It is hard to imagine his ever choosing to escape, but in an ironic twist, it was precisely his deeply rooted sense of obligation to others that eventually led to his greatest achievements. He was able to reimagine the call of duty he had felt within his family in the public realm. Yet his thoroughgoing commitment to upstanding behavior and righteous causes was not without its personal costs. For many years there remained about him something

of the precocious boy, and if some aspects of his emotional development were neglected or stifled, it was perhaps the inevitable consequence of his singular family drama. However, he brought away from his unusual youth uncommon powers of focus and execution, and the habit of hard work. His standing at the bank, his blossoming affinity for art and culture, and his egalitarian spirit combined to win him universal respect. In 1881 he married Frances Kinsley, daughter of the city's best-known restaurateur (FIG. 11). One year later, he finished building a large Queen Anne–style house on that most elegant of residential streets, Prairie Avenue. This was Charles Hutchinson as he embarked on the long adventure of his involvement with the Art Institute of Chicago.

FIGURE 10. Hutchinson, c. 1877. Even as a young man, he was an effective and disciplined executive. His friend Hamlin Garland noted in a posthumous appreciation that although "his most familiar gesture was pulling his watch from his vest-pocket," he always exuded a friendly warmth.

FIGURE 11. Frances Kinsley as a young woman, before her marriage to Hutchinson. The eldest daughter of Herbert M. Kinsley, Chicago's most prominent caterer, she was a graduate of the prestigious Dearborn Seminary. Intelligent and adventurous, Frances was a vivacious hostess who avowed she had "acquired the art of talking and listening at the same moment." The couple met when both were teachers at the Burr Mission, a chapel and Sunday school at the corner of Wentworth Avenue and 23rd Street. Chicago History Museum, ICHi-21398.

"A BRICKS AND MORTAR MAN"

THE PROPERTY THE TRUSTEES purchased at the corner of Michigan Avenue and Van Buren Street was an ideal site for the museum and school, looking across to the lakefront and easily accessible from many parts of the city. It was sold to the Art Institute for $45,000, well below its market value, by the financier Sidney Kent. In later years, this discount was attributed to the intercession of board member James H. Dole, but as Kent was a longtime partner of Benjamin Hutchinson and a large stockholder in the Corn Exchange Bank, it is probable that Hutchinson was instrumental in negotiating the favorable price. The lot had already been improved with a commercial building, in which the museum established its first quarters. A brick addition was erected on the rear of the lot to house more galleries and rooms for the school.

Hutchinson understood the impact of brilliant occasions and organized a lavish evening reception to open the new museum. The planning committee, perhaps uncertain of the response, issued four thousand invitations. The recipients, however, understood it to be a major event. Although the card did not specify formal clothes, many guests appeared in full evening dress, and the halls were crowded for the entire four-hour party. On view were the best pictures owned by the group (only a few in number), including its latest acquisition: *Beheading of Saint John the Baptist*, a large, florid Salon painting by the Boston artist Charles Sprague Pearce.[1] The main attraction was a substantial loan exhibition of over one hundred oil paintings and watercolors from local private collections. Probably the finest of these was lent by Marshall Field: Jean-François Millet's *Harvest Moon*, a small, compressed composition depicting a peasant woman walking at twilight. Other highlights were works by Rosa Bonheur, Adolphe-William Bouguereau, Frederic Edwin Church, Jean-Baptiste Corot, Ernest Meissonier, Adolph Schreyer, and Constant Troyon. The press delighted in the opportunity to dissect the seldom-seen holdings of Chicago's most prominent citizens. Generally eager to be supportive, the *Chicago Tribune*'s critic was unable to resist a gibe at Levi Leiter, who had recently presented some works from his collection to the Metropolitan Museum of Art in New York, noting "L. Z. Leiter sends a small and rather disappointing sheep picture by Rosa Bonheur."[2] Following the gala, the museum remained open to the public without charge for a week, after which nonmembers could visit for an admittance fee of one quarter. In the excitement of the inaugural festivities, the Art Institute sold enough annual memberships to eliminate its $5,000 deficit.

Later that same month, another major attraction was announced. Four tapestries from the Gobelin workshops, woven from designs by Charles LeBrun, would be installed in the galleries for the month of February (FIG. 2). Part of a series of eleven hangings depicting scenes from the life of Alexander the Great, they were owned by the Civil War general Philip H. Sheridan. Initially reluctant to permit even a mild cleaning and then sustained exposure under skylights, Sheridan was persuaded by Hutchinson that their display would help generate public interest in the new museum.[3] In fact, the tapestries drew so many visitors that their stay was extended by two weeks.

FIGURE 1. Central stair and hall of the Art Institute's first custom-built home on Michigan Avenue. The structure was designed by the firm of Burnham and Root in the Romanesque Revival style then popular among cultural organizations; it also featured modern conveniences such as an elevator to transport visitors to the top floor.

FIGURE 2. Advertisement for one of the new museum's first exhibitions, a show of Gobelin tapestries woven from designs by Charles Le Brun, court painter to Louis XIV.

FIGURE 3. The Chicago Art League, a group of young, locally trained male artists, was invited to hold its annual exhibition at the new museum. Some time later, the female artists of the Bohemian Club were extended a similar invitation.

Over the next few years, Hutchinson dominated both policy decisions and practical matters, expending much effort and imagination to help create a regular and varied exhibition schedule that would appeal to a wide range of tastes. Paintings, engravings, and sculptures were borrowed, singly or in groups, from museums and collectors. Landscapes tended to dominate, with some good works on view by Corot, Albert Bierstadt, Jules Breton, Charles-François Daubigny, and Thomas Moran. An unusual but popular departure was the 1885 show of delicate Art Nouveau illustrations by Elihu Vedder for the first illustrated edition of the *Rubáiyát of Omar Khayyám*. Hutchinson was in his element the evening it opened, standing at the entrance to the main gallery, surrounded by patrons and artists, "the embodiment of genial dignity."[4] More informal shows featured such subjects as Christmas cards, posters, and photographic reproductions of paintings and sculptures in the great museums of Europe. A group of original illustrations from the *St. Nicholas* and *Century* magazines were placed on permanent loan.[5] The contribution working artists made to the young institution's atmosphere of hope and excitement should not be underestimated. Many groups, including the Chicago Art League, the Bohemian Art Club, the Chicago Pottery Club, and the Western Art Association, were offered rooms for annual exhibits (FIG. 3). These shows of contemporary work, together with the activities of the Art Students League, brought a good deal of color and spirit to the museum, especially when their programming included celebratory suppers and some modest cash prizes.

* * *

As Hutchinson assumed a commanding role, the position of William M. R. French (FIG. 4), who had adopted the title Director of the Art School in the summer of 1880, was still uncertain. French was born in 1843 into a distinguished New Hampshire family. He was the son of Henry Flagg French, a lawyer, assistant secretary of the treasury, and first president of the Massachusetts Agricultural College (later the University of Massachusetts). His brother was Daniel Chester French, a sculptor already famous for his statue *The Minute Man* in Concord. French attended Phillips Exeter Academy,

FIGURE 4. William French's carte-de-visite, c. 1873. Proud of his distinguished New England roots, French wrote a fellow graduate, "I presume you know I am a Harvard man—class of '64." Chicago History Museum, ICHi-61252.

artistic, industrial, and scientific displays (FIG. 5). At some point, French also began teaching at the Academy of Design, eventually becoming its secretary. When the trustees resigned from this group, French sided with them and subsequently served as chief administrator of the new organization. He always described this transition as "a painful period" and for a long time was troubled by the perception that he had abandoned his fellow artists.[7] Two years later, French's life was disrupted by the death of his young wife, Sarah. Apparently suffering a breakdown, he left Chicago before the start of autumn classes in 1881.

As part of his recovery, French spent some years abroad, studying and visiting many European museums and art galleries. In his absence, his duties were performed by Newton H. Carpenter, a young teacher of perspective who had been connected with the Academy of Fine Arts since its inception. In 1883 Carpenter was officially named secretary, a position he held for over thirty years, effectively serving as the Art Institute's business manager. When French returned to Chicago in 1884, he was named director and also resumed his role as head of the school. By this time, however, Hutchinson was accustomed to arriving at the museum by nine in the morning and supervising its every routine, including the choice of exhibitions, the arrangement of pictures and display cases, and all manner of decisions relating to gifts, loans, and purchases. These responsibilities were later shared with two or three additional trustees, comprising an art committee, with French acting in an advisory capacity. This administrative pattern continued indefinitely. While French was in firm command of the school and its affairs, his authority at the museum was circumscribed from the start, and over time he came to accept that condition as inevitable given the nature of the job.

* * *

Rich in good will and admiration, the museum nevertheless had yet to receive many donations of either artworks or money. What is sometimes called its first gift—a marble replica of *The Lost Pleiade* by the American sculptor Randolph Rogers (FIG. 6)—was received in February 1883 from Elizabeth Hammond Stickney and exhibited with Sheridan's tapestries.

graduated from Harvard, and moved to Chicago a few years later to begin a career as a civil engineer and landscape architect.[6] He wrote for journals, taught classes such as the one Hutchinson and his friends stumbled on, and increasingly focused his energies on art, serving as manager of the Inter-State Exposition's art department. First proposed by Potter Palmer the year after the Great Chicago Fire, when the city was struggling to rebuild its morale and commercial standing, the Inter-State Exposition was an immediate success and came to be an annual event, with its last installment in 1890. Held in a hastily erected hall on the lakefront at Adams Street (where the Art Institute now stands), it featured a wealth of

FIGURE 5. Constructed in 1873 on the lakefront at Michigan Avenue and Adams Street, the Inter-State Exposition Building housed popular artistic, industrial, and scientific displays. It was demolished in 1891 to make way for the Art Institute's second structure on Michigan Avenue, the present Allerton Building. Chicago History Museum, ICHi-38555.

Stickney later presented her late husband's collection of engravings and etchings as well. These were first housed in the Art Institute's growing library and later transferred to form the nucleus of a small print department. In 1884 subscriptions were solicited to pay for a large collection of casts of Assyrian, Egyptian, Greek, Roman, and Renaissance sculptures, to be purchased abroad. At about this time, Addie M. Hall Ellis wished to create a memorial to her first husband, who had been an ardent member of St. Paul's Universalist Church, the Hutchinsons' congregation. She made a large contribution toward this project, and thereafter the entire group was known as the Elbridge G. Hall Collection. But Ellis's was the only substantial donation of cash. Many chances to acquire important works while they were still affordable

were thus lost, although probably some mistakes were avoided as well.[8]

However limited its ability to acquire works of art, by January 1885 the museum was already running out of exhibition space for its growing collection. The trustees decided to buy the vacant lot immediately to the south and considered extensively remodeling the existing structures. Instead, after some discussion, Hutchinson asked prominent architect John Wellborn Root to prepare plans for a new building that would give the Art Institute a far more impressive presence on Michigan Avenue. This meant once again taking on substantial debt. During the summer the lot was secured, and Hutchinson, as chair of the building committee, raised $22,000 in subscriptions, along with generous agreements

FIGURE 6. Randolph Rogers's *The Lost Pleiade*, 1874—75, in a vintage postcard, c. 1905. While in Rome, Elizabeth Hammond Stickney purchased the sculpture from the artist himself. She first loaned and then presented it to the new museum. Stickney also donated her late husband's collection of engravings and etchings, and later bequeathed $75,000, the first large cash gift the Art Institute received. Collection of Celia Hilliard.

perspective rendering, asking "my dear Mr. Hutchinson" to "please criticize it freely."[10] By September they had agreed on working drawings for a handsome five-story building in the Romanesque style, clad in rough pink-brown sandstone, with an arched portal, great rounded windows, massive towers at the corners, and decorative medallion busts of famous artists (FIG. 7). When it was finished in autumn 1887, its interiors displayed the museum's holdings to good advantage, provided ample space for loan shows, housed club rooms for sympathetic organizations, and even offered an area in the attic for artists' studios. Of the thirteen exhibition rooms, four were occupied by the cast collection, which illustrated the whole range of Western sculpture, and three more were hung with the museum's own paintings (FIG. 1). Six additional galleries were reserved for loan exhibitions. Upstairs more galleries (and some of the stairways) were hung with

FIGURE 7. The Art Institute's Burnham and Root building at Michigan Avenue and Van Buren Street, completed 1887. Built of Connecticut brownstone and red Colorado sandstone, its Romanesque Revival design featured rough-faced masonry, corbelled turrets, and relief portraits of Leonardo, Michelangelo, and Raphael near the peak of the front facade. Chicago History Museum, ICHi-02228. Photograph by C. D. Arnold.

from contractors to donate $18,000 in labor and materials.[9] Hutchinson himself (or the Corn Exchange Bank) furnished the balance needed to start construction until the museum could sell $100,000 in bonds to finance the project.

The firm of Burnham and Root, noted for integrating modern construction methods and materials and neoclassical design, was just entering its most productive period. Their Montauk Building, finished in 1882, had been called the first true skyscraper, and plans were already underway for the Rookery Building at LaSalle and Adams streets. Hutchinson maintained close friendships with both men, and in fact it was Root who in 1882 had designed the simple structure on the Michigan and Van Buren lot to house the school. By July 1885 Root was already sending revisions of a large-scale

FIGURE 8. Jean-François Millet (French, 1814–1875). *Peasants Bringing Home a Calf Born in the Fields*, 1864. Oil on canvas; 81.1 x 100 cm (31 ¹⁵/₁₆ x 39 ⅜ in.). Henry Field Memorial Collection, 1894.1063.

engravings, illustrations, and prints. The Society of Decorative Art had business quarters and showrooms on the second floor.[11] Rooms were also rented to the Fortnightly of Chicago, the Chicago Literary Club, and the Chicago Woman's Club, groups that brought additional intellectual and civic activity into the building and sometimes provided direct support for museum or school projects. The rents they paid also helped to defray the expanded Art Institute's increased operating expenses.

* * *

The doors to these imposing quarters opened at a gala celebration in November 1887. A full orchestra was stationed on the second floor, lemon frappe was served from silver trays, and a great crush of guests spread out through the building, eager to explore all of its magnificently appointed rooms. On view were a group of paintings loaned from Chicago and elsewhere. Most of the critical attention focused on *Peasants Bringing Home a Calf Born in the Fields* by Millet, which Henry Field, a brother of Marshall Field,

had recently acquired (FIG. 8). But the featured exhibition was a trove of diplomatic souvenirs belonging to the late Elihu B. Washburne, who had served as minister to France during the Franco-Prussian War and the Paris Commune. It was an impressive assemblage of autograph documents, engravings, photographs, and historical portraits (including a full-length depiction of Kaiser Wilhelm, a personal gift from the emperor himself). Only a portion clearly belonged in an art museum, even by the more elastic standards of the day. Nevertheless, Hutchinson had arranged for the whole collection to remain on long-term loan, with the apparent hope of luring a wider audience into the new building by appealing to popular taste. In another such effort to attract diverse visitors, a lavish Salon painting, *The Last Hours of Mozart*, by the Hungarian artist Mihály Munkácsy, was exhibited in December. First shown in the galleries of Chicago's Calumet Club, where the public had thronged daily to admire it, the picture was so popular that its move to the Art Institute was announced in the papers alongside ads for the South Side Dime Museum and St. Jacob's Oil, a neuralgia remedy. Upon viewing this melodramatic canvas, the critics, whom Hutchinson courted with the same meticulous attention he applied to all aspects of the museum's welfare, magnanimously allowed, "No one will be the worse for seeing it."[12]

The institution continued to offer a mix of elite and popular attractions with the intent of encouraging loans, drawing crowds, and enlisting new members. The following year it imported from London a superlative collection assembled by the late George W. Reid, keeper of prints in the British Museum. On view were one hundred prints, many in very rare and early states, and about 175 drawings attributed to such masters as Annibale Caracci, Correggio, Donatello, Bartolomé Esteban Murillo, Rembrandt van Rijn, and Peter-Paul Rubens. Hutchinson visited the dealer Louis Ehrich in Connecticut and persuaded him to loan his entire collection of Dutch and Flemish pictures, most of which had been held for some time in Yale University's art department. Selections from the private collections of Chicago continued to line the walls. Among the most frequent local lenders were Samuel M. Nickerson, a founder and president of the First National Bank; George M. Pullman, inventor of the railroad sleeping car; and Philander C. Hanford, an early stockholder of the Standard Oil Company and owner of works attributed to Hans Holbein, Murillo, Rembrandt, and Titian. The Art Institute received some gifts as well.[13]

Many shows were accompanied by descriptive leaflets, and the museum published the first official catalogue of its holdings in 1888. At the same time a serious library was being formed. Originally a conglomeration of books cobbled together for the use of students in the school, the facility was now housed in comfortable quarters of its own (FIG. 9) and drew substantial donations to support the purchase of important illustrated books and reference materials.[14] For example, Eadweard Muybridge's pathbreaking, sixteen-volume *Animal Locomotion* cost $600 and was bought with subscriptions from Hutchinson, Addie M. Hall Ellis, and others. The museum hosted weeklong symposia on Dante and Shakespeare. Public lectures by notable figures in art and architecture (such as architects William LeBaron Jenney and Louis Sullivan, and sculptor Lorado Taft) and visiting professors added to its growing scholarly reputation.[15]

However, the attraction that exceeded all attendance records was the 1889 Vasily Vereshchagin exhibition (FIG. 10). The Art Institute's first real blockbuster, its popularity seemed to stem from both its lurid subjects and the heated press commentary it generated. The show featured many of this Russian realist's colossal battle scenes—vast canvases depicting sensational images of misery and gore.[16] The artist said that his intention was to advance the cause of peace by illustrating the atrocities of war. Debates about the merits of his work raged in the papers, and some critics claimed Vereshchagin's true artistry was found only in his small, quiet nocturnes. The crowds poured in regardless. The six-week show, briefly extended, was visited repeatedly by existing Art Institute members and drew 601 new ones. On free days, the museum was packed, and another 4,263 people paid full one-time admission fees.[17] Some of the Art Institute's chief benefactors deplored the show as pure bathos, but none could deny it had happily tested the capacity of the museum

FIGURE 9. The Art Institute's library, on the second floor of the Burnham and Root building. At first a basic study collection, due to the generosity of donors it came to encompass rare volumes, important reference works, and periodicals, as well as books for circulation among the students.

FIGURE 10. Invitation to the members' preview of a one-man show by the prolific Russian artist Vasily Vereshchagin, whose work depicted the horrors of war. The exhibition attracted controversy and drew thousands of visitors, making it the Art Institute's first blockbuster.

and roused a new level of interest. By spring, the coffers sufficiently sturdy, Hutchinson reported to the trustees that negotiations were underway to lease additional gallery and lecture space on three floors of the new Studebaker Building, then under construction just south of the museum.

* * *

Indeed, as the Art Institute grew, the ambitions of local collectors rose as well. More exhibitions were held all over the city, new periodicals expanded coverage of the art market, and "the Chicago connoisseurs" developed a reputation for their powers of discrimination and the fervor with which they sought works they admired.[18] Some of this activity was undoubtedly stimulated by the annual art shows at the Inter-State Exposition. Under the astute direction of longtime manager Sara Hallowell (FIG. 11), the six galleries devoted to art soon outstripped all other attractions in quality and attendance. For several years they featured mostly American work. A supportive art committee (on which Hutchinson served for a time) assured the availability of loans from local citizens and dealers. Much was also imported from galleries and studios elsewhere. For many visitors, these shows were their first opportunity to become acquainted with trends and developments in contemporary art. For those who could afford to buy, it was an important source, and for those who established ties with the influential Hallowell, it opened broad new worlds of collecting. Most famously, Hallowell kindled the enthusiasm of Bertha Honoré Palmer, who went on to invest heavily in the work of the French realists, the Barbizon School, and the revolutionary Impressionists then just beginning to win recognition.

The Chicago collecting community was, however, a rich and varied patchwork of interests, tastes, and motivations. Hutchinson maintained cordial relations with almost everyone, but throughout his life he preferred the company of charismatic scholars and well-versed connoisseurs to that of rich trophy hunters. Among these was the flamboyant public transit king Charles T. Yerkes, who liked to publicize his quest for European masterworks and acquired canvases by Jean-François Millet, Van Dyck, Rembrandt, and Rubens.[19] He may have been the first American to purchase a work by Auguste Rodin, and later loaned the Art Institute that sculptor's 1893 *Orpheus and Eurydice* (now a prize possession of the Metropolitan Museum of Art, New York). By contrast, Henry Field, who had spent part of his retail career in Paris and preferred "to stay at home with his soul," brought back paintings by Millet, Corot, Troyon, Eugène Delacroix, and

FIGURE 11. Sara T. Hallowell, manager of the art department at the Inter-State Exposition, in a sketch by Anders Zorn published in *Art Amateur*, June 1893. Despite a petition signed by Hutchinson, French, and others to appoint Hallowell head of fine arts at the 1893 World's Columbian Exposition, she was only given responsibility for assembling its loan collection. She later moved to France and served as the Art Institute's Paris agent until the start of World War I. The Newberry Library, Chicago.

Théodore Rousseau.[20] Nor was Bertha Palmer the only buyer with courage to experiment. Edson Keith, an early trustee, also purchased a Claude Monet landscape from the Inter-State Exposition in 1890. Robert Hall McCormick was assembling a group of fine English pictures from the Tudor era forward. Cyrus McCormick, the Deerings, the Pullmans—all made a vocation of buying well, refining their collections, and establishing Chicago as an important art center in America.[21]

Perhaps the city's most colorful collector was James W. Ellsworth (FIG. 12), who, having amassed a large fortune from coal mining operations in Pennsylvania and West Virginia, turned his prodigious energies to building a major art collection that included works by Ralph Blakelock, Frederic Edwin Church, Winslow Homer, George Inness, and Eastman Johnson, as well as ancient coins, Chinese porcelains, Greek figurines and vases, Japanese ivories, and Mexican pottery. His accomplishments as a connoisseur were recognized in 1887, when he was elected a governing member of the Art Institute. A few weeks later proposed to the trustees that they establish an annual juried exhibition of American oil paintings. They accepted his suggestion, along with his offer to set aside a sum from which a $300 prize could be offered in perpetuity to the best picture not previously exhibited in the Midwest by an artist currently working in the United States. The museum supplemented this award with a second prize of $250, to be given to any American artist, whether working at home or abroad. In order to increase the number of entries from the East Coast, the museum announced that it would cover transportation and insurance costs, sale prices would be printed in the catalogue, and any transactions would be free of commission. The first Annual Exhibition of American Oil Paintings opened in May 1888. It was an enormous success and garnered much national attention. The show, which was repeated for many years to come, emerged as the centerpiece of the museum's exhibition schedule.

Were there anyone who might have wished to challenge Hutchinson's perennial reelection as president of the board of trustees, or who conceived of himself as a likely successor, it was Ellsworth. In June 1888 he was voted onto the board of trustees, and the following autumn he offered to guarantee the expense of opening the museum, free of charge, on Sunday afternoons. He then decided to widen the scope of his own collection, starting with Rembrandt, and managed to spirit *Portrait of a Man* away from its owner, the Princess de Sagan, a French aristocrat in need of ready cash.[22] His collecting adventures became a staple of the city's art columns. In December 1889, he arranged for Millet's painting *The Angelus*, which had been sold to the American Art Association for a large price at the famous Secretan sale in Paris that summer, to be shown at his own house for two weeks in advance of its display at the Inter-State Exposition. He then commenced to build a new and much grander home on South Michigan Avenue that some called a shrine to his Rembrandt.[23] At the same time, Ellsworth declared that he would loan his entire collection to the Art Institute for an indefinite period. He may thereafter have expected a certain level of recognition that was, however, not forthcoming. For

FIGURE 12. James W. Ellsworth was a millionaire coal mine operator, art collector, member of the World's Columbian Exposition board, and erstwhile trustee of the Art Institute. Flamboyant and in love with the hunt for paintings as much as the works themselves, he was the only man who could have challenged Hutchinson's position as president of the museum's board of trustees.

whatever reasons, after the annual meeting of the trustees in June 1890, he abruptly resigned. Perhaps it is not surprising, given his character, that Hutchinson remained on friendly terms with Ellsworth for the rest of his life, although he was always wary of the latter's impulsive, grandiose style. During the World's Columbian Exposition, Hutchinson granted Ellsworth the freedom to sometimes act on his behalf as chair of the local art committee, only to later learn Ellsworth had assured foreign governments that any rare art they assented to loan would be transported across the seas on United States warships.[24]

Hutchinson was never a particularly adventurous or ambitious collector on his own behalf, but he bought art of many periods and styles for close to forty years. He began at an early age, motivated in part by a desire to create a comfortable home environment for his family and by his affinity for a learned atmosphere. During his youth, his family occupied two adjoining houses on Harrison Street. They were two adjoining houses on Harrison Street. They were connected inside, and young Charles had the entire top floor of one to himself. Years later Frances Hutchinson recalled her first visit to her future husband's rooms, with their leatherbound books, beautiful china, fine furniture, and carefully chosen etchings and engravings.[25]

In 1878 Hutchinson accompanied his mother and sister Nellie on a journey to London and Paris, where he purchased art pottery, richly painted china, and a watercolor by a "Miss Coleman" in a gold frame and mount. On a trip to New York the following summer, he made more serious visits to Hermann Wunderlich and Company (later Kennedy Galleries) to buy about two dozen drawings and etchings, including at least one by James McNeill Whistler. He visited local dealers as well and sometimes bought work from the Inter-State Exposition. At this point, his collection included pieces by Chicago artists such as Lawrence C. Earle, Oliver Dennett Grover, Leonard Volk, and Annie C. Shaw, the first female member of the Academy of Fine Arts. His status as an art patron was sufficiently well known in Chicago that French approached him for a donation to the Academy of Design. "He looked doubtful," as French recounted some years later, "and gave me $50"—a moment of generosity that is often cited as the beginning of Hutchinson's long years of devoted service to the Art Institute.[26]

Once installed as president of the museum, he began

FIGURE 14. George Frederick Watts (English, 1817–1904). *Time, Death and Judgment*, 1866. Oil on canvas; 91.5 x 72 cm (36 x 28 5/16 in.). Bequest of Charles L. Hutchinson, 1925.724.

to collect both more, and more expensive, work, focusing mainly on Anglo-American portraits and atmospheric landscapes. He purchased several canvases by Albert Fitch Bellows and paid a good price for *The Last Minstrel* by George H. Boughton, a London-born artist who lived in Albany and painted American colonial genre scenes. Then, in 1886, he bought Jules Dupré's *Cows in a Stream* from the New York dealer William Schaus. Dupré was a widely accepted, fashionable Barbizon painter, but the purchase represented

FIGURE 13. David Teniers the Younger (Flemish, 1610–1690) after Paolo Veronese (Paolo Caliari) (Italian, 1528–1588). *Abraham's Sacrifice of Isaac*, 1654/56. Oil on panel; 20.9 x 30.7 cm (8 1/4 x 12 1/8 in.). Gift of Mrs. Charles L. Hutchinson, 1936.123.

FIGURE 15. Dante Gabriel Rossetti (English, 1828–1882). *Beata Beatrix*, 1871–72. Oil on canvas; 87.5 x 69.3 cm (34 7/16 x 27 1/4 in.). Charles L. Hutchinson Collection, 1925.722. When Hutchinson purchased this canvas in 1886, some critics thought it was probably the only painting by Rossetti in an American collection. Its rarity and value notwithstanding, Hutchinson frequently loaned the picture to other museums and galleries.

FIGURE 16. John Melhuish Strudwick (English, 1849–1937). *Isabella and the Pot of Basil*, 1879. Tempera with gold paint on canvas; 99.7 x 69.8 cm (39 ¼ x 27 ½ in.). The De Morgan Centre, London. © The De Morgan Centre, London / The Bridgeman Art Library.

expensive. He then traveled to London that summer (apparently alone) to visit Bond Street dealers and view works going to auction the following autumn. In this way he acquired, through Thomas B. Agnew and Sons, three small but masterful canvases by David Teniers the Younger—copies of Italian paintings by Giorgione, Titian, and Veronese owned by Teniers's patron, Archduke Leopold Wilhelm of Austria—that had been created as models for engravings (FIG. 13).

On the same trip, Hutchinson also embarked on what must have been an exciting clandestine adventure in pursuit of works by the celebrated painter George Frederick Watts. His art seldom came on the market, but after the recent death of Charles Rickards, a businessman who had been his main patron, there was to be a massive sale. Indeed, it is possible that the opportunity to view this collection had been the primary reason for Hutchinson's voyage. Certainly Watts's allegorical pictures held a strong moral and intellectual appeal for him. Concerned with large themes like faith, hope, judgment, and time, they suggested the triumph of spiritual realities over the grimy conditions of the industrial age. Once in London, Hutchinson discovered that the pictures were still at Rickards' house in Manchester. Nevertheless, an employee at the Grosvenor Gallery arranged for him to see them, instructing him to go to that city and discreetly contact a Miss Chesworth at Seymour Square, Old Trafford. "She is his cousin," the man explained. "I have written to tell her you will call . . . Some of the paintings are very beautiful . . . Please take note of any that may especially strike you . . . Kindly be precise in your notes so that I may have no doubt about the pictures you refer to, and also kindly avoid any reference to the sale in speaking to Miss Chesworth."[27]

The actual sale at Christie, Manson and Woods, which included fifty-seven works by Watts, took place the following April, at which time Hutchinson bought a portrait of the renowned violinist Joseph Joachim, a much-acclaimed study in lights and shadows that Watts had painted in a second version for Rickards.[28] Some years later, Hutchinson acquired another Watts canvas, *Time, Death and Judgment*, the epitome of the heavily symbolic compositions the artist hoped would ensure his reputation (FIG. 14).

While Watts may have been his intended quarry on the 1886 trip, when Hutchinson visited the London galleries, he found himself fascinated by another trend in English art. The Grosvenor Gallery had that winter hosted a one-man exhibition of the work of John Everett Millais, one of the founders of the Pre-Raphaelite Brotherhood, a group of British painters who rejected academicism in favor of working from life and looked to medieval art for inspiration. Hutchinson quickly paid £100 for an enigmatic canvas, *Isabella and the Pot of Basil* (FIG. 16), by John Melhuish Strudwick, an artist who began his career in the studio of Edward Burne-Jones, another Pre-Rphealite. It was based, like many of the movement's works, on a literary source: John Keats's poem "Isabella; or the Pot of Basil" (from a story by Giovanni Boccaccio), a tale of thwarted love that had already inspired major paintings by Millais and William Holman Hunt.

This acquisition was only a prelude, however, to the boldest purchase of Hutchinson's career (FIG. 15). At Agnew's he was shown Dante Gabriel Rossetti's startling canvas *Beata Beatrix*, a dramatic rendering of the poet Dante Alighieri's great love as she sits in a trance, resplendent, receiving the symbolic warning of her imminent death: a crimson bird drops a white poppy into her hands, while a nearby sundial indicates the hour of her passing. In the distance are the sorrowing figures of the poet and a personification of Love. Rossetti first painted this image in 1863, a year after the suicide of his wife, Elizabeth Siddal, who was clearly his model for Beatrice. In 1872 he completed a copy of the painting for his friend William Graham, to which he added a predella showing Dante and Beatrice reunited in paradise. This later version, which was mounted in a gold frame of the artist's own making and shown in the Rossetti memorial exhibition at the Burlington Fine Arts Club in 1883, was the one offered to Hutchinson.

Richly colored and suffused with an unmistakably erotic glow, *Beata Beatrix* is unlike any picture Hutchinson bought before or after. Given the enduring influence of his early religious education, he was probably attracted to the picture's theological associations, and may have seen in the figure's rapture a moment of sacred revelation or celestial import. Certainly he understood it was a strong and important work, and an opportunity to acquire a major painting by an artist of indisputably high standing. He paid over £1,200 for it (about $4,000 at the time), making one of his largest art investments to date.

Beata Beatrix arrived in Chicago later that autumn but was not displayed at the Art Institute until the following

FIGURE 17. William Holman Hunt (English, 1827–1910). *The Triumph of the Innocents*, 1876–87. Oil on linen; 157.5 x 247.7 cm (62 x 97 ½ in.). Walker Art Gallery, Liverpool. © Walker Art Gallery, National Museums Liverpool / The Bridgeman Art Library.

year, when the 1887 Burnham and Root building opened. It caused a big stir, drawing both praise and criticism. "The picture is at once engaging and repellant," noted the *Chicago Tribune*'s critic, a conclusion echoed in the national press.[29] At that time the Pre-Raphaelites were not well known outside England, and American collections contained very few examples of their work. But whether or not *Beata Beatrix* was viewed favorably, it excited attention. Moreover, Hutchinson continued to admire the work of Rossetti and his peers and, perhaps seeking to further the movement's success, two years later arranged for Holman Hunt to display his sensational canvas, *The Triumph of the Innocents* (FIG. 17), in Chicago. The eight-foot-long painting depicted the Holy Family on the flight into Egypt, surrounded by flocks of toddling cherubs representing the children slaughtered by Herod. In advance of its exhibition, it appeared in a full-page engraving in *Harper's Weekly*, and the popular New York clergyman and critic Henry Van Dyke declared it "the most important religious picture of the century."[30] But to local eyes its conception seemed bizarre, its bright, clear colors too harsh, and the gurgling infants positively offensive.[31] Holman Hunt, who had probably hoped to sell the work to the Art Institute, pointed out in his defense that at first the Pre-Raphaelites had been regarded as heretics but that their pictures were

FIGURE 18. The Fine Arts Building at the World's Columbian Exposition. Designed by Charles B. Atwood, the neoclassical temple was restored from 1929 to 1940 and reopened as the Museum of Science and Industry. Chicago History Museum, ICHi-02228.

now "praised by the sons of those who stoned the prophet in his youth."[32]

Hutchinson's enthusiasm for this kind of work persisted. In 1894 he made one more significant Pre-Raphaelite acquisition, purchasing a large wash drawing by Burne-Jones. Titled *Flora* and dated 1888, it is a colorful cartoon, or model, for a tapestry. Executed in various shades of violet with gold hatching, the drawing may have reminded him of his beloved *Beata Beatrix*.

* * *

Hutchinson once observed, in a seeming echo of Daniel Burnham's famous adage "Make no little plans," that in all the public institutions of Chicago, the same mistake had been made time and again: the plans were laid on too small a scale and "hampered . . . the growth that was sure to come."[33] Approaching the final decade of the century, having established a secure foothold in the city's cultural landscape and having won its citizens' allegiance, the museum found itself in a surprising predicament. Its handsome Burnham and Root building, paid for through bonds sold to the museum's most loyal supporters, was only three years old but the organization—exceeding its highest expectations—had already outgrown it.

Yet to build again, to reach so soon for a vastly larger place on the national stage, was felt to be an audacious move.

Just at this moment, however, an opportunity appeared that seemed unlikely to return. That extraordinary chance came in the guise of the World's Columbian Exposition, a triumphant celebration that would make Chicago, at least temporarily, a world capital. It was decided that such a fair must have an art exhibition space worthy of a great city. Therefore, funds, land, and legislative support would be available that might disappear in ordinary times. In retrospect, given these fortuitous circumstances, the building of the Art Institute's Renaissance palazzo on the lakefront seems inevitable. In fact, it was a feat that required quick judgment, tenacity, and a talent for political maneuvering that would test the mettle of even as seasoned a captain as Hutchinson.

In February 1890, after a fevered competition, Chicago was named the host city for the exposition. Jackson Park, on the South Side, was appropriated as the central site for the fair, but the first plans also called for a series of structures on the lakefront, the only acreage designated for erecting buildings of a permanent character. The assurance that some enduring memorial would in fact remain standing after the fair did much to bolster public support. In September the city passed an ordinance granting the fair the use of the lakefront land,

FIGURE 19. The Art Institute under construction, 1892. Designed by Shepley, Rutan and Coolidge, the building first housed the World's Congress Auxiliary during the World's Columbian Exposition. The E-shaped structure was separated from the lakeshore by the tracks of the Illinois Central Railroad..

and the owners of contiguous property on Michigan Avenue signed an agreement permitting this arrangement, pending two conditions: that the Illinois Central Railroad remove or sink its tracks, and that any buildings situated south of Jackson Boulevard would later be demolished.

Hutchinson immediately moved to secure one of these lakefront structures for the Art Institute. In his capacity as chairman of the fair's fine arts committee (a position his rival Ellsworth had also coveted), he roused the formal support of the prestigious Commercial Club at a banquet organized to affirm that the exposition should benefit the city's art galleries and museums.[34] During that autumn, an "art building" was assigned to the lakefront and plans were undertaken to make it a central feature of the fair. There was talk of spending as much as $1,000,000 (the equivalent of nearly $124,000,000 today) to create it.

At a special meeting of the Art Institute's governing members in December, John Root showed sketches of a proposed museum, a rectangular two-story edifice—an ample, ornamental building designed to impress, with a winged staircase and a dome in the center.[35] To Hutchinson and his contemporaries, this neoclassical Beaux-Arts design (and the different structure that was eventually built as the Art Institute's permanent home) embodied two seemingly

FIGURE 20. The Art Institute opened to the public in its new home on December 8, 1893. It was at once a monument to the World's Columbian Exposition and the beginning of a new era in the cultural life of Chicago.

unexpected death from pneumonia the following month all the more unfortunate. By this time his partner, Burnham, had been named the fair's chief of construction, and Root's drawings for five lakefront structures (including art and decorative art buildings, a music hall, an ornamental waterworks, and a pavilion for electrical displays) were, for the time being, set aside. In the following months, it became apparent that negotiations with the railroad were headed toward a problematic compromise, and in any case new objections arose to building on the lakefront. Potter Palmer in particular wished to know what the city would receive in exchange for giving up four blocks of prime real estate, putting Burnham "in high feather" over the possibility of a less than satisfactory settlement.[36] By early March, the exposition directors talked of relinquishing the lakefront site altogether.

Hutchinson, sensing there was no time to be lost, quickly turned to the city council, courting the aldermen who could round up the necessary votes to cement the museum's claim to lakefront property. This was artfully managed, and in March an ordinance was passed whereby the Art Institute acquired a site. The city granted parkland to the museum in perpetuity, on which was to be erected a building that the World's Columbian Exposition would control for the duration of the fair. In return, the Art Institute agreed to adhere to its stated mission, to include the mayor and comptroller as ex-officio board members, and to permit specified hours of free public access. This triumph was followed just two months later by another, when Hutchinson carried his motion for a $200,000 appropriation from the Exposition Company, which proposed to use the museum's building during the fair for the World's Congresses Auxiliary, which would host lectures and conferences "across all departments of thought" on subjects including commerce, education, medicine, philosophy, religion, science, and many humanitarian causes. This meant,

different structure that was eventually built as the Art Institute's permanent home) embodied two seemingly contradictory ideas. Its size, formal symmetry, and sculptural details invoked the European tradition, declaring the museum worthy of standing alongside the older cathedrals, monuments, and palaces of Western civilization. At the same time, the fact that this lavish building would be open to the public made clear its thoroughly modern, democratic mission of displaying for all classes of society the treasures previously reserved for the elite. Root's designs were well received, making his however, that the fair's own art exhibition space would likely be relocated to Jackson Park, an idea that met with mixed reactions. The fair's art director, Halsey Ives, was strongly opposed, as he worried that the South Side gallery would divert resources from the permanent project on the lakefront. Nevertheless, in June the exposition directors voted to place the entire artistic portion of the fair in Jackson Park, in a building to be designed by Charles B. Atwood based on John Root's sketches. Many lamented that almost $600,000 would be diverted to create this temporary structure (FIG. 18). But to Hutchinson, the shining prize had been won: the splendid site on the lakefront was the museum's.

The battle did not end there. At first things proceeded smoothly. The Art Institute was able to sell its building at Michigan and Van Buren to the Chicago Club for $425,000, raising the bulk of the money it needed to build its new structure, and the Inter-State Exposition finally endorsed the proposal, which ended all litigation over its eminently desirable site at the foot of Adams Street. In October the Boston firm of Shepley, Rutan and Coolidge won the design competition for the permanent building. This pleased Hutchinson, who had developed a close friendship with Charles Coolidge during the years he supervised construction of the Glessner House on Prairie Avenue, a distinctive, thick-walled dwelling designed for John and Frances Glessner, close friends of the Hutchinsons. Matters were proceeding so well that Charles felt comfortable departing on a four-month trip at the end of December 1891. In January, work began (FIG. 19).

However, as a reporter described it, "No sooner is Mr. Hutchinson out of town and off for Europe than a scheme is broached to strangle the promising infant." Various factions who felt excluded from "the art palace conspiracy" worked to "throttle that malignant plan."[37] One such plot gained traction. Sara Daggett, who owned property on Michigan Avenue, came forward to object that her view of the lake would be obscured. There was some confusion as to whether her husband, in signing the consent form, had perhaps gone beyond his authority as her agent. In spite of a public outcry, Daggett was granted an injunction, and all work on the partially erected building stopped. Emergency meetings were called. The trustees considered petitioning the city for a site north of Washington Street, but no action

was taken. To complicate matters, at the governing members' annual meeting in June, three well-regarded trustees spoke in favor of moving the whole Art Institute project to Jackson Park. They succeeded in passing a motion to that effect, authorizing the arrangements necessary to make the change. Hutchinson, recently returned from his travels, may have expressed disappointment or frustration to close friends but remained silent in public.

A hearing was held in late June, and it was understood that the decision of the judges would be final, appeal being of no avail for lack of time. Witnesses were called, and Daniel Burnham was forced to acknowledge that the trustees had proceeded with construction even though they had been apprised beforehand that Daggett would object. Her attorney argued that the City of Chicago never actually held the park's land, except in trust for the people, and therefore had no right to grant it.

The hearing lasted several days. Edwin Walker, solicitor general of the World's Fair Company and a hardy veteran of the Chicago bar, made the closing argument on behalf of the museum. He built his case on the ground that the Illinois State Legislature had granted the city permission to make agreements with the World's Columbian Exposition and to retain rights to some permanent structures. The facts that the Inter-State Exposition Building had stood for seventeen years on the very same site, and that property values were now expected to increase and not diminish, added weight to his reasoning. The following day, the injunction was dissolved.

The stoppage inflicted an extra $25,000 in construction costs, but work resumed immediately and the Art Institute's lakefront building was hurried to completion in time for the fair's opening day on May 1, 1893 (FIG. 20). In January 1894, at the first annual trustees' meeting held in the new structure, Walker, having perhaps set a new standard for "eminent services," was elected an honorary member of the museum. Hutchinson, meanwhile, had consolidated his position as the undisputed "father" of the Art Institute. First among equals and the organization's effective head of state, he enjoyed a near universal support that sustained him in office for the next thirty years.

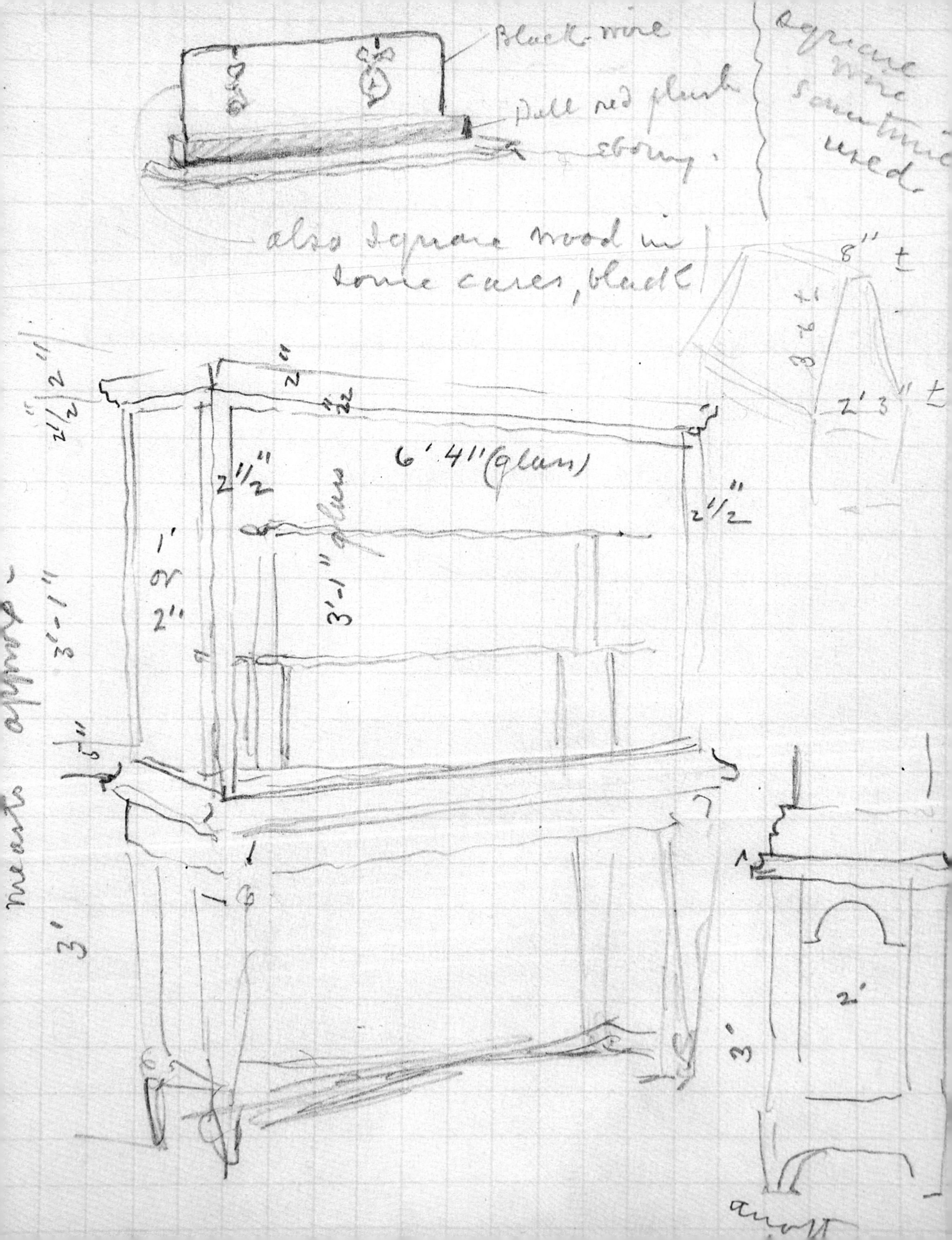

black wire

Dull red plush
ebony.

square
wire
sometime
used

also square wood in
some cases, black

8" ±

3' 9" ±

2' 3" ±

2"

2"

2½"

6'·4" (glass)

2½"

2"½

2½"

8" glass

1'
0'
2"

3'-1" glass

3"

2½"½

3'-1" apart

means apart

3'

7

6

3'

2'

3'

"PICTURE EXCITEMENT"

MANY GREAT MUSEUMS are noted for the buildings they inhabit, but ultimately their quality rests on the excellence of their collections and the skill with which they are presented. Thus, during this same period when the grand new home for the Art Institute was in gestation, Hutchinson also turned his attention to issues of interior design and presentation, and considered what purchases and gifts might best augment the museum's growing reputation. In 1889 and 1890, he made two important journeys that exerted a lasting influence on the direction of both his own life and the Art Institute's future.

In March 1889, Hutchinson sailed to Europe (FIG. 2) accompanied by his wife, Frances, and William French, who recorded their explorations in a red leather pocket diary that remains one of the Art Institute's most prized archival documents (FIGS. 1, 8). Like many upper-class Americans of the time, the three travelers visited Paris, Rome, Florence, Venice, and London. However, this was more than a Grand Tour, for the men intended to build relations with kindred institutions while studying European trends in museum display and art instruction. They also carried pledges of monetary support should they find objects and pictures worthy of purchase. For French, who had not been abroad since his long trip at the start of the decade, it was an important opportunity to acquire expertise and contacts that could help expand his role at the museum. He noted with pleasure in a dispatch home, "The relations which we have formed with artists and connoisseurs in Paris are likely to be useful."[1]

Hutchinson's concentrated focus on practical matters, so typical of his approach to all aspects of life, enabled these two dedicated museum men to absorb a wealth of European perspectives and know-how in a short amount of time. Perhaps of more importance in the long run, however, was Hutchinson's renewed admiration of Classical antiquity and the revival of his ambition to fill the Art Institute with works that could best represent the world's highest artistic achievements. This expedition undoubtedly inspired his later trips to Egypt, where the ruins and relics of the ancient world never failed to seize his imagination. Compared to its temples, he once wrote, "all other buildings seem like toys."[2]

Over a period of two months the group toured such institutions as the Musée du Louvre, the Musée des Arts Decoratifs, the Borghese Palace, the Sistine Chapel, the Vatican (FIG. 4), the Uffizi, the South Kensington Museum (now the Victoria and Albert Museum), and the Wallace Collection. French's notebooks are filled with sketches of display cases, fountains, mosaic-tile floors, pedestals, skylights, staircases, and wrought-iron doors (FIG. 1). He measured benches, collected wallpaper samples, and made notes on conservation treatments. The Hutchinsons and French observed with some pride that their own organization's quarters in Chicago compared favorably with spaces and appointments in the new Musée du Luxembourg. In Paris they also visited a dozen of the Art Institute's own students and teachers on sabbatical abroad, who gave firsthand accounts of instruction and examination methods at the École des Beaux-Arts and other government schools. French concluded that the teaching techniques and facilities in Chicago were in some ways superior but did not deny the "indefinable atmosphere of art" that enveloped the studios of Paris.[3]

FIGURE 1. Detail of French's travel diary for April 27, 1889, showing a sketch of a display case in the South Kensington Museum (now the Victoria and Albert Museum) with measurements. During his 1889 European tour with Hutchinson, French took copious notes and made many sketches of objects and fittings in the museums they visited, so that they could better furnish the Art Institute's own galleries upon their return.

FIGURE 2. Frances and Charles Hutchinson aboard ship, likely on their way to Europe, c. 1904. After Hutchinson transferred official control of the Corn Exchange Bank to his colleague Ernest A. Hamill in 1898, he and his wife traveled abroad for several months almost every year.

FIGURE 3. Hutchinson, a lover of ancient cultures and their artifacts, first visited the Roman Forum in 1889. He returned on his fiftieth birthday, in 1904, when this snapshot was likely taken.

FIGURE 4. The Hall of Statues at the Vatican Museum, 1880/1900. While visiting these galleries in 1889, French—always on the lookout for ways to display the Art Institute's own burgeoning collections to best advantage—carefully noted their Pompeian red walls and unglazed tile floors. © Michael Maslan Historic Photographs / CORBIS.

FIGURE 5. Greek (Attic). Attributed to the Chicago Painter (his Name Vase). *Stamnos* (Wine Jar), c. 450 B.C. Terracotta, red-figure technique; h. 37 cm (14 ⅝ in.); diam. of handles: 41.9 cm (16 ½ in.); diam. of rim: 21.1 cm (8 ⁵⁄₁₆ in.). Gift of Philip D. Armour and Charles L. Hutchinson, 1889.22.

In Rome the group wandered the Baths of Caracalla, the Colosseum, and the Forum (FIG. 3). The party was given a warm reception by Rodolfo Lanciani, the government director of excavations, who promised to help steer them to high quality, authentic Greco-Roman pottery. After examining the wares of several dealers, Hutchinson and French selected many exceptional objects, mostly red-figure earthenware dating from 470 to 300 B.C. These included bowls, drinking cups, plates, vases, and water jugs, all notable for their elegance of line, simple decoration, and beautiful varnish. An especially rare find acquired at this time was a *stamnos* (wine jar) depicting preparations for a Dionysian festival (FIG. 5). The men also purchased a few Roman marbles. Hutchinson bought some objects for his personal collection but, following his emerging funding strategy, the costs of articles destined for the Art Institute were shared among various donors. As French once described it to a reporter, Hutchinson "has a great knack of getting things for the public good by inviting some rich man to give half while he gives the other half."⁴ In this way he was able to hunt and acquire continuously on behalf of the museum, giving within his own means while at the same time

building a loyal and committed base of donors. Long before the advent of professional development officers, Hutchinson recognized the importance of attracting support from many quarters.

Near the close of their tour, the group returned to Paris to attend the Exposition universelle. A celebration of the hundredth anniversary of the storming of the Bastille, this great fair was an ode to the Third Republic and its burgeoning industrial might. The controversial new Eiffel Tower served as centerpiece and entryway, and among the event's numerous attractions was a magnificent art gallery featuring works from all over the world (FIGS. 6-7). Many prominent Chicagoans wandered this international salon, including Bertha and Potter Palmer. Earlier, in Rome, Hutchinson had crossed paths with Philip D. Armour, who authorized the purchase of a picture in his name, and helped fund the acquisition of the *stamnos*. Although they had taken copious notes on many paintings for sale by dealers and auction houses, Hutchinson and French chose for this gift a canvas displayed at the exposition, *The Shepherd's Star* by Jules Breton (FIG. 8). French liked to recall his quiet delight at spotting Breton himself in the gallery one day.

When the trio returned home, the men saw to it that the antiquities they had purchased in Italy were displayed in new cases of the style and size they had seen abroad. For Hutchinson these objects were the inspiration for a new commitment to ancient art. Later that summer he wrote to the Archaeological Institute in Cambridge, Massachusetts, proposing a collaboration. Its president, Charles Eliot Norton of Harvard University, sent his colleague William Cranston Lawton to make a presentation in October at the Lake Shore Drive home of Franklin MacVeagh, a banker and fellow sponsor of the initiative. Lawton exhorted support for the Archaeological Institute's planned excavations at Delphi (with an implicit promise to share the spoils among institutional contributors). In December the Art Institute became a dues-paying member of the group. In February Hutchinson brought to the museum Amelia Edwards, the English traveler and founder of the Egyptian Exploration Fund. He and French had met her in London the previous year. Edwards made an extraordinary impression on the audience, and the Art Institute joined her organization too,

FIGURE 6. During their visit to Paris, the Hutchinsons and French visited the Exposition universelle, which could be entered via a promenade around the newly erected Eiffel Tower. CORBIS.

FIGURE 7. Interior of the Fine Arts Building at the Exposition universelle, 1889. The exposition drew many visitors from Chicago, including the Hutchinsons, French, Philip D. Armour, and Bertha and Potter Palmer. Note the similarity between its arrangement and that of the Fine Arts Building at the World's Columbian Exposition (p. 49, fig. 3), held in Chicago approximately five years later. CORBIS.

with each of its executive committee members agreeing to be individual patrons as well. Hutchinson expressed his personal passion for the ancient world in an evocative remembrance of his 1889 journey titled "Ecco Roma."[5]

❊   ❊   ❊

Another highlight of the 1889 trip had been a visit to Pratolino, near Florence, to view the late Prince Anatole Demidoff's collection of Dutch and Flemish Old Master paintings. Impressed with their high quality, Hutchinson returned to Europe the following winter with the principal mission of borrowing all or some of these works for a show at the Art Institute. French, who had recently remarried and was setting up house in Beverly, a neighborhood on Chicago's Southwest Side, did not participate in this trip. The Hutchinsons instead planned to join their Chicago friend Martin Ryerson, a man who would play an important role in this and all museum matters long into the future.

By his own account, Hutchinson greatly needed rest after several years of strenuous effort to further both his business career and fulfill his civic responsibilities. "I scarcely realized how near a total wreck I had become," he wrote in a journal at the time.[6] He had a "fit of the blues" so severe that he began to wonder if "after all we had made a mistake in undertaking the World's Fair." At first the trip offered no respite. Out of sorts, he complained that the S. S. Champagne was a "roller" and not nearly so good as last year's ship. Frances, always prone to be seasick, remained in her stateroom, leaving Charles to roam the deck, where he chatted with a woman he took to be Louise Chandler Moulton, a well-known poet of the day. When the poet was called to recite after dinner, she was not the same person at all. "Good joke on me," he wrote in his diary,

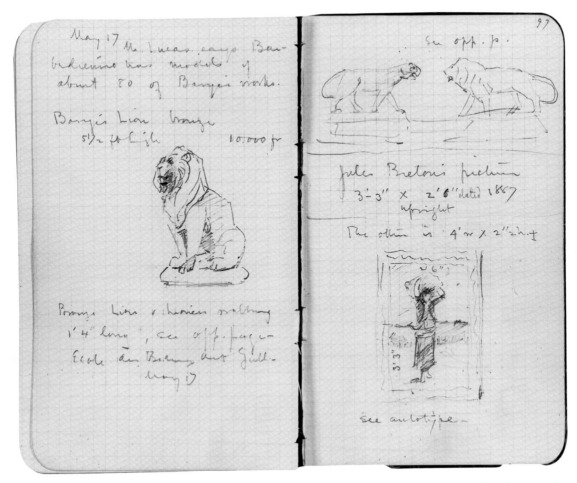

FIGURE 8. A spread from French's travel diary for May 17, 1889. When Hutchinson and French encountered Philip D. Armour in Rome, he instructed them to "purchase a good picture in his name." In Paris, after considering many options, the pair settled on Jules Breton's *Shepherd's Star,* which was on display at the Exposition universelle. French's sketch of the work is visible at bottom right; at top right and at left can be seen lion sculptures from the École des Beaux-Arts that may have inspired those that would later flank the Art Institute's entrance.

adding that anyhow the imposter had not come up to his expectations. He enjoyed the band concert given to raise money for a seamen's home but lamented that "even in mid-ocean one cannot escape from the continual call upon one's generosity for sweet charity's sake." However, Hutchinson was subsequently able to ease into a relaxed mode unlike any he had known before, which established for him a lifelong connection between travel abroad and freedom. Although this was his fourth trip to Europe, it was the first time he had the leisure to take in ordinary amusements and cosmopolitan pleasures. Arriving in Paris, he and Frances went riding in the Bois de Boulogne, saw Sarah Bernhardt in *Jeanne D'Arc,*

and mailed a postcard from the top of the Eiffel Tower. The couple dined in cafés with friends from home and even met Hutchinson's old literature teacher, Mrs. Meatyard, who now maintained an artists' salon. She introduced them to the painter Elie Delaunay, from whom Charles commissioned a portrait of Frances on the spot. A few weeks later, the Hutchinsons left for Spain, where they visited cathedrals, lush gardens, the Alcazar, and the Alhambra. They went to the bullfights ("disgusting except the final work of the Matadores") and attended an antique show ("where I was tempted to almost bankrupt myself"). Everywhere they went, Frances took snapshots with her new Kodak. She was especially

FIGURE 9. In the late 1880s, the Hutchinsons and Ryersons, then in their early thirties, bonded in a deep friendship that endured for the rest of their lives.

engaged by the donkeys, the street peddlers, and the women and children who followed her and Charles everywhere, showering compliments and asking for pennies. "After being told yesterday that I was the most beautiful man in the world," Hutchinson recorded, "I was quite prepared for anything. One old lady at the Carthiza told me I had a face like a bishop. Of course, she received two coppers."

As always, tours of museums were central on the agenda. In Paris, Hutchinson was still in awe of the Louvre, although this time he decided it was hung too densely, remarking, "The collection would be so much more satisfactory if one-half of it was removed." He was disappointed to discover so little of old Spain in Madrid but found the Prado "beyond description." He had never seen paintings by Murillo, Ribera,

or Velázquez before and made four visits to the museum in two days.

As previously arranged, the Hutchinsons met up in Granada with Ryerson and his wife, Carrie, whom they were coming to know very well. Martin was at this time managing his late father's lumber fortune and just emerging as a civic leader in his own right. Reportedly, he and Hutchinson discovered their shared love of art at a dinner party one evening, and a social acquaintance blossomed rapidly into a profound friendship (FIG. 9).[7] Ryerson had been elected a governing member of the museum in 1887 and had begun to collect, most notably textiles. Part of his youth had been spent abroad with his parents, which perhaps endowed him with a certain sophistication. When he and Hutchinson visited the antique shops in Madrid a few days later, undoubtedly it was Ryerson who selected some exceptional tapestries and embroideries for the museum's collection.

Upon resettling in Paris at the Normandy Hotel with their wives, the men addressed the main task of their journey: securing the Demidoff loan. The Demidoff family were among the great nineteenth-century collectors, having assembled a fabled group of masterpieces over the course of two generations.[8] In the 1870s, Prince Paul Demidoff brought together various excellent Dutch pictures, which he put up for auction in 1881. The sale did not bring high prices, and thirty of the best works were bought in. He died shortly thereafter, and his wife, Princess Elena, went to live in Russia, while the pictures remained sequestered in the family villa at Pratolino. In the late 1880s, a small group was sold; these works eventually came to hang in the Museum of Fine Arts, Boston. At some point the princess decided to sell the rest of the collection and engaged the Parisian dealer Durand-Ruel as her agent.

Thus when Hutchinson and Ryerson arrived at the Durand-Ruel gallery expecting to negotiate a loan, they instead heard about prices. Some fine paintings were gone already, and it was abundantly clear that if the museum had any intention of buying the best that remained, the two men would have to act quickly. It was a big risk, as financing the purchase required trusting in personal pledges and the museum's future revenue. However, the assured provenance of the works was persuasive. At the time, given the limited analytic techniques available, if an Old Master painting did not have a known ownership history, even the most expert scholars were hesitant to verify its authenticity. Accordingly, as Hutchinson reported later, "I cabled the situation to Mr. Field, Mr. Armour, Mr. Kent, and a few others. I asked them to buy the pictures and to hold them till such time as the Art Institute was able to buy them, or until generous men could be found to donate them. They promptly gave us authority to buy them, and we went down to Florence and closed the sale. We secured thirteen pictures for about $200,000. A year ago they could not have been had for twice that sum."[9]

The purchase included paintings by Anthony van Dyck, Frans Hals, Meindert Hobbema, Rembrandt, Peter Paul Rubens, and Jan Steen (FIG. 10).[10] Along with the Demidoff

pictures, Hutchinson and Ryerson also acquired through Durand-Ruel a fourteenth work for the museum—*Portrait of a Man with a Pink*, then attributed to Holbein and now credited to Quentin Massys. While still in Paris, they happened to meet trustee Edson Keith, who promptly made the first gift in support of the acquisition, purchasing Willem Van Mieris's canvas *The Happy Mother*.

That spring the foreign correspondent for the *New York Times* reported that all Paris seemed flush with "picture excitement."[11] Enjoying the euphoria of buying, Hutchinson and Ryerson quickly made important purchases for their own collections. While still at Durand-Ruel, Hutchinson bought two magnificent sixteenth-century panel paintings, the wings of an Adoration triptych by an Antwerp Mannerist (FIG. 11), and a pair of portraits by Nicolaes Maes. Ryerson acquired three pictures, including Cornelis Huysmans's *The Hollow Road*, a landscape once in the Demidoff collection.[12] From the auction of bibelots owned by Eugene Piot (an early photographer and world traveler) they carried off several cases of antiquities, including ancient terracotta figurines from Tanagra, Greece, and iridescent glass bottles and vases from southern Italy, Phoenicia, and Syria. For one lot they happily outbid the Louvre, causing much consternation and an editorial rebuke from *Le Figaro*.

News of the Demidoff purchase was met with a mix of genteel condescension and scornful jeers on the East Coast. The *New York Press* suggested that Hutchinson had probably picked the biggest paintings and "paid $1,000 a front foot for them," after which he would no doubt be carried along the lakefront in "a huge triumphal float led by milk-white Berkshire hogs," gibes that alluded to stereotypes of Chicago as an uncivilized frontier town plagued by unrestrained growth and dominated by the meat-packing industry. Hutchinson may have deliberately played to these prejudices. On his return to the United States, as he came down the gangplank in New York, he assured the swarm of reporters who had met his ship that the pictures were "corkers, every one of them."[13]

The Art Institute's Demidoff paintings were placed on exhibit the following November. Ignoring the insults of the Eastern press, Chicagoans reveled in the splash and glamour of this masterly coup. The museum's annual report declared

FIGURE 10. Meindert Hobbema (Dutch, 1638–1709). *The Watermill with the Great Red Roof*, 1662/65. Oil on canvas; 81.3 x 110 cm (32 x 43 ¼ in.). Gift of Mr. and Mrs. Frank G. Logan, 1894.1031. This canvas and *Young Girl at an Open Half-Door* by the workshop of Rembrandt were the two costliest paintings in the 1890 Demidoff purchase.

the acquisition "the most important step of the year," not only for Chicago but for all of America. Over the next few years, the cost of this daring purchase was partly covered by a handful of generous individuals, including Hutchinson (who presented the Hals) and Ryerson (who donated the Rembrandt). But as the years passed and the initial excitement was transferred to newer ventures, further donations were few and far between. The final payment for the last unfunded painting was not received until the 1930s.[14]

The Demidoff acquisition and its subsequent display bestowed on the Art Institute an international reputation. It set a new standard for the exhibition and acceptance of Old Masters and, together with the building of the handsome structure on the lakefront, firmly established the museum as a suitable repository for art of the highest caliber.

FIGURE 11. Antwerp Mannerist (Master of the Antwerp Adoration Group) (Netherlandish). *King David Receiving the Cistern Water of Bethlehem* (left) and *King Solomon Receiving the Queen of Sheba* (right), 1515/20. Oil on panel, transferred to canvas; 73.5 x 27.5 cm (28 ⅞ x 10 ⅞ in.), 73.2 x 27.7 cm (28 ⅞ x 10 ¾ in.). Gift of Mrs. Charles L. Hutchinson, 1936.127, 1936.126.

"A COMMITTEE OF TWO"

HAVING INSPIRED A BURST of civic enterprise, the World's Columbian Exposition, held during the spring and summer of 1893, was an extended art exhibition in itself. Its neoclassical white pavilions, surreal statuary, and glittering lagoons were hailed as the embodiment of an ideal city and as marking the emergence of a more cultured American society. The world-class works on view at the Fine Arts Building in Jackson Park seemed to confirm that Chicago had shed its provincial past (FIG. 3). The eighty galleries contained creations spanning several centuries, although the three great modern movements—Romanticism, the Barbizon School, and Impressionism—dominated. The displays included works in all media by both new and established artists. Architecture was represented by a large collection of casts from the Musée Trocadero in Paris. But art from all over the world could also be seen throughout the fairgrounds, including, in the Women's Building, a spectacular display of work by female painters and sculptors assembled by Bertha Palmer. Many Chicago connoisseurs later attributed the earliest inspiration for their collecting to sights and treasures they first encountered at the fair.

As chairman of the fine arts committee, Hutchinson was in his element. Once again, his organizational abilities and refined sensibility served him well. He assisted Greece in arranging the display of ancient marbles at its national exhibit and, in recognition of this aid, was appointed its consul general in Chicago, a title he retained for some years. The nation's display, which also featured such native products as honey, oils, olives, soaps, sponges, and wines, won forty-six awards. King George of Greece was exceptionally pleased by this and later anointed Hutchinson a Knight Commander of the Order of Our Savior, a decoration established in 1829 when the country was recognized as an independent state. During the exposition itself, Hutchinson hosted a string of visiting artists, dignitaries, and intellectual celebrities at festive evenings, often assisted by Halsey Ives, exuberant head of the fine arts department. To one of his many summonses, Ives replied, "All right . . . I'll put on my silk hat in honor of the occasion . . . And by thunder! I'll have my trousers done up in a dude crease."[1]

According to plan, during the fair the new lakefront home of the Art Institute was adapted for use by the World's Congress Auxiliary, and many Chicagoans first entered its doors to attend an event in one of two mammoth lecture halls constructed in the center of the building (FIG. 4). Perhaps the most memorable address given there was Swami Vivekananda's tribute to Hinduism and yoga, delivered on the opening day of the World's Parliament of Religions. His simple greeting at the podium, "Sisters and brothers of America," brought the audience of thousands to its feet for a three-minute ovation, a testament to the fervent interest in non-Western spirituality then sweeping the nation. Another great occasion was historian Frederick Jackson Turner's presentation of his pathbreaking paper, "The Significance of the Frontier in American History," in which he argued that the American character had been decisively shaped by the struggle to conquer the West.

When the Art Institute took over the building at the close of the fair, the lecture halls and other temporary rooms were torn out. Although it would be several years before the center and rear of the structure were completed, the interior

FIGURE 1. The Hutchinsons and Ryersons were intrepid travelers, adapting with enthusiasm to exotic locales such as the tropical forests of Sri Lanka, which they visited in winter 1896.

FIGURE 2. Jules Breton (French, 1827–1906). *The Song of the Lark,* 1884. Oil on canvas; 110.6 x 85.8 cm (43 ½ x 33 ¾ in.). Henry Field Memorial Collection, 1894.1033. This painting, part of the first major gift prompted by the Art Institute's new Shepley, Rutan and Coolidge building, was often reproduced on postcards and posters, and was voted the most popular painting in America at the *Century of Progress* exhibition that accompanied the 1933 World's Fair.

cious galleries that featured crimson and maroon walls and were illuminated by glazed skylights overhead. These rooms had been designed in response to the arrangements French and Hutchinson had seen during their tour of European galleries, after which they were preoccupied with the proper architectural proportions of exhibition spaces and, above all, the problem of lighting. As French once observed, "Our theory is that it is easy to shut out light, but hard to get it in." He believed that while paintings could be effectively exhibited with broad overhead illumination, sculpture required sidelights.[2] Accordingly, when plans were later made to expand the museum by building across the railroad tracks, the space on the bridge was intended as a long gallery for the museum's now large assemblage of casts, and the size of the windows was adjusted to admit less light from above.

Just as Hutchinson had hoped, this palatial new home had already inspired a major donation. Henry Field's widow, Florence Lathrop Field, announced in June 1893 that she would give the museum her late husband's collection, which was composed mostly of Barbizon pictures, including important works by Millet and Delacroix, as well as Jules Breton's popular *Song of the Lark* (FIG. 2). To honor the Field Collection, it was housed in a special memorial room with a glass mosaic canopy custom designed by Tiffany and Company. Furthermore, when Hutchinson proposed that two bronze lions be commissioned to flank the steps of the museum, Field offered to cover the cost of this project as well, although on condition that the lions be designed by Edward Kemeys, an animal sculptor whom her husband had admired and known personally.[3] Soon other gifts began to flow in: individual paintings, sets of engravings and etchings, embroideries, silver, and statuary. Collectors were generous with loans, and a regular schedule of special exhibitions was established. The modest but significant library was growing, and the school was thriving. The Art Institute was now firmly positioned to take its place at the center of cultural life west of the Alleghenies (FIG. 5).

Throughout this period, as Hutchinson worked to strengthen the museum and increase its influence, he was also in the process of reordering the other parts of his life. Up to this point he had focused on his business affairs, specifically on running the Corn Exchange Bank, where he served

spaces were reconfigured according to Shepley, Rutan and Coolidge's original plans. The first floor was almost entirely devoted to the museum's large cast collection, which had recently been supplemented by works donated and purchased from the Musée Trocadero, and facsimiles of antique bronzes found at Herculaneum and Pompeii; the latter were given by Harlow N. Higinbotham, Hutchinson's good friend and the head of the World's Fair Company. On the second floor, the corridors were lined with carved wood furniture; glass cases displaying pottery, textiles, and other objects presented by the Society of Decorative Art; and suits of armor recently shown in the German "castle" at the exposition. The Art Institute's growing collection of paintings was hung in spa-

FIGURE 3. Interior of the Fine Arts building at the World's Columbian Exposition. For thousands of visitors, this exhibition was their first opportunity to view the work of artists they previously knew only by name. The similarity between its arrangement and that of the Fine Arts Building at the Exposition universelle (p. 40, fig. 7), held in Paris approximately five years earlier, is probably not coincidental, for Hutchinson, the chairman of the fine arts committee for the Chicago exposition, had visited the Parisian fair. Hubert Howe Bancroft, *The Book of the Fair* (Bancroft Company, 1895), vol. 3, p. 670.

who dreamed of living the life of the mind rather than entering the business world, and he served as its very active treasurer to the end of his life.

Sometime in the early 1890s, Hutchinson decided to free most of his time for involvement in public affairs, travel, and aesthetic pursuits. He later explained that he simply wished "to live a little easier," and the choice was clearly a reflection of his deepest inclinations, but it is likely that his resolve to change course was reinforced by witnessing his father's financial ruin.[5] Benjamin Hutchinson was at the height of his fame when he engineered the great wheat corner of 1888. He purchased vast quantities of the staple crop at less than $1 a bushel and then, when the crop was unexpectedly damaged by frost, he ran the price up to $2, forcing devastating losses on other traders, including some of his oldest friends. Thereafter he engaged in a round of furious speculation until he himself was caught on the wrong side of the market in a deal that ended his career. This coincided with an apparent decline of his mental faculties, and he was mercilessly fleeced by those whom he had previously bested.

as president. He had many other financial interests as well. He was a longtime director of the Northern Trust Company, the State Bank of Chicago, the Traders Insurance Company, and several corporations controlling the city's surface and elevated rail lines, and in 1888 he was elected president of the Chicago Board of Trade. For some years he managed these weighty commercial responsibilities alongside a growing list of civic commitments, which often consisted of heading young institutions in search of major funding. For example, in 1890 he played a crucial role in founding the new University of Chicago, which at that time needed significant support from the local business community to match John D. Rockefeller's large initial donation (FIG. 6). Luckily, the organizers of the school discovered that Hutchinson's endorsement of their endeavor opened doors all over the city. As Thomas W. Goodspeed, secretary of the first board of trustees, recalled, his "was a name to conjure with."[4] Hutchinson, in turn, found in the University of Chicago an enlightened institution almost as compelling as the Art Institute. It may have appealed to that part of him that was still a young man

FIGURE 4. Columbus Hall in the Art Institute's new building, 1893. For the duration of the World's Columbian Exposition, the structure was used by the World's Congress Auxiliary, which erected two large, temporary lecture halls on the north and south ends of the main floor. Hubert Howe Bancroft, *The Book of the Fair* (Bancroft Company, 1895), vol. 3, p. 922.

FIGURE 5. The sculpture hall in the new Art Institute was popular with visitors of all ages. French once overheard a little girl, staring up at the cast of the Farnese Hercules, ask her mother "if it was Roosevelt."

of Trade was a fundamental benefit to the American farmer and in a certain light could even be seen as a philanthropic institution. This had inspired hoots of laughter from the elder Hutchinson, who saw no higher meaning in his activities. Surrounded the next day by a gaggle of brokers, he pointed to each one of them and cried, "You're a gambler, and you're a gambler, and I'm a gambler!"[7] These widely divergent perspectives suggest the gulf that existed between father and son. Benjamin's funeral was attended by both foes and friends, including the captain of the first boat on which he ever loaded grain. Charles was in California when he received word of his father's death and immediately boarded a train for home but did not arrive in time for the service or burial.

The circumstances of Benjamin's decline meant that Charles did not inherit a fortune comparable to those of the city's wealthiest families. But he had built prudently on his early advantages to amass substantial assets of his own and could readily afford to withdraw from everyday involvement in business. Accordingly, he began to shift the active management of the Corn Exchange to his colleague, Ernest A. Hamill. A grain trader and protégé of Benjamin Hutchinson, Hamill was conservative, strikingly handsome, and a very able financier. Hired as vice-president in 1889, he was not officially named head of the organization until nine years later, when it was reorganized under the new national banking laws, and he and Hutchinson simply exchanged titles. In 1900 the Corn Exchange absorbed the American National and Northwestern National banks, making it the second largest financial institution in the city with respect to deposits. Two years later, it took over the Merchants National as well. Hutchinson, of course, still held almost four times as many shares as Hamill and was involved in all major matters, including the 1906 decision to build an imposing bank and office tower at the northwest corner of Adams and LaSalle streets. Hamill, however, was largely responsible for the strong and steady growth of the Corn Exchange, which throughout this period paid an annual dividend of

Reportedly, an accountant hired to review his books found only $50,000 in assets. It was also rumored that Charles had begun legal proceedings to appoint a conservator unless his father promised to quit trading.[6] Over the next few years, the elder Hutchinson intermittently disappeared, only to be found wandering the streets of Evansville, Indiana (ostensibly on his way to Florida), running a shabby saloon in New York, and, finally, operating a junk shop near the Brooklyn Bridge. Eventually he was brought home and placed in the Oakwood Sanitarium in Lake Geneva, Wisconsin, where he spent the remaining years of his life. Throughout this period, he showed no signs of regret or repentance, carrying himself with a trace of defiance and rebuffing any hints of pity or condescension.

When Benjamin Hutchinson died in 1899, his glory years were resurrected in obituaries that dominated the newspapers for several days. At the Rialto Building, his old stomping grounds, friends and acquaintances reminisced about his dazzling career. One man recalled that Charles Hutchinson had once given a speech declaring that the Board

FIGURE 6. Hutchinson served as treasurer of the University of Chicago from its inception in 1890 until his death in 1924. In 1901 he gave $60,000 to build Hutchinson Commons, a neo-Gothic student dining hall. Special Collections Research Center, University of Chicago Library.

FIGURE 7. The Hutchinson home at 2709 South Prairie Avenue, after 1888. Originally a red brick structure designed in the Queen Anne style, it was remodeled in the French Gothic mode seen here.

twelve percent and formed the core of Hutchinson's prosperity. Over the years "Ernest and Charley" (as they were affectionately known in the city's business district), developed a close personal friendship. They were regular patrons at Rector's Oyster House and scarcely missed a major theatrical performance, whether a Shakespeare play or the operetta *Babes in Toyland*. They saw the famous vaudevillian Eddie Foy in *Mr. Bluebeard* at the Iroquois Theater two nights before the infamous fire that claimed over six hundred lives.

Hamill was also Hutchinson's neighbor on Prairie Avenue, where Charles had remodeled his house into the haven of art, literature, and hospitality that he had always desired (FIG. 7). This sanctuary was itself surrounded by relatives and friends in an enclave that the Hutchinson family had virtually established in the early 1880s. The northern, upper portion of exclusive Prairie Avenue was largely developed after the Chicago Fire, when prominent men such as Marshall Field, George Armour, and George M. Pullman built homes there. Just to the south was an area known as Carville, a jumble of cottages, shops, and warehouses, all remains of

a railroad car industry that had failed when some nearby stockyards moved inland. "Lower" Prairie Avenue started at 26th Street, the location of St. James Catholic Church, built to serve the mostly Irish population that had worked the yards of Carville. In 1880, after the congregation relocated to Wabash Avenue, Benjamin and Charles Hutchinson bought a large portion of its land.[8] They immediately resold two lots to the families of Charles's sisters, and later other parcels were purchased by friends and business associates. In 1881 architect George O. Garnsey, who had done much work for Benjamin in other parts of the city, designed a Queen Anne–style house on an oversized lot for Charles and Frances, who had just married. In what was probably a reflection of his affinity for religion, Charles chose for his own home the precise address of the frame building where St. James had first been established.

Among the couples' closest friends were John and Frances Glessner, fellow members of the city's social and civic elite. When the Glessners built their house, a Romanesque fortress designed by Henry Hobson Richardson, at the corner of Prairie Avenue and 18th Street, Hutchinson—not one to

FIGURE 8. Prairie Avenue between 26th and 27th streets, c. 1892. Although one of Chicago's finest residential neighborhoods, it retained a peaceful, small-town feel, especially on this particular stretch. Chicago History Museum, ICHi-61110. Photograph by Chas G. Whitson.

modify his aesthetic standards, even for friends—was among those who first indulged, as Frances Glessner wrote in her diary, in "some rather rugged criticisms."[9] However, on touring its interior, he was reportedly "enthusiastic over everything," particularly its charming library and "home-like air."[10] In January 1888, at the Glessners' invitation, he brought over his own architect, Francis M. Whitehouse, to study its layout. Son of the Episcopal bishop of Illinois, Whitehouse had designed residences and several church structures, and had recently completed the new St. Paul's Universalist Church at Prairie Avenue and 30th Street, a commission undertaken at Hutchinson's behest. Now Hutchinson engaged Whitehouse to enlarge and remodel

his own home in the French Gothic style. The architect was responsible for the exterior of the design, but it is likely that a good deal of the interior decoration and some of the furnishings were created by Francis Bacon. An architect and designer, Bacon had worked in Richardson's office before moving to A. H. Davenport and Company, manufacturers of furniture that interpreted the ideals of the Arts and Crafts movement in high-quality machine-produced items. Bacon's work featured fluid carving and naturalistic motifs. He shared Hutchinson's interest in antiquity, having spent two years at the archaeological excavations at Assos in Turkey. At the close of the remodeling, he sold the Art Institute a superior collection of ancient Roman coins and terracottas.

FIGURE 9. Frances Glessner, one of Hutchinson's closest friends, in her conservatory, dressed for a Benvenuto Cellini–themed dinner party. Glessner was an accomplished silversmith herself and made two hand-hammered pieces for the Hutchinsons' silver wedding anniversary in 1906. She also shared Charles's love of horticulture. An avid beekeeper, she sometimes sent him boxes of fresh honey on the comb, one of his favorite treats. Chicago History Museum, ICHi-061818.

Hutchinson, like Richardson, believed that a home should be a total aesthetic environment. His paintings were hung throughout the dining, music, and reception rooms, but most attractively in the library, which was probably his favorite place in the house. The painter and critic Kenyon Cox, who assessed Hutchinson's collection for a scholarly catalogue, described the library as a low-ceilinged space with book-lined shelves, broad tables covered with papers and magazines, and wide windows looking out over a well-kept lawn and garden.[11] Hutchinson had a good collection of antiquarian books and fine modern bindings, which he encouraged visitors to handle, and he hung smaller paintings low, where they could readily be taken from the walls for closer study. He continued to purchase exotic furnishings

during his travels all over the world and was especially enthusiastic about painted porcelain and tableware, from Delftware to Doulton and meat plates to tureens. Frances Hutchinson noted, however, that to the end of her husband's life they used the same Wedgwood blue breakfast set that he had selected at the age of sixteen "if ever he should marry."[12]

The couple kept a small domestic staff, but Charles clearly delighted in managing the household affairs himself, deciding on new carpeting or a change in color scheme, or puttering in the garden, cutting flowers and arranging them as well. "I am a lover of flowers," he said once. "It is a taste I inherited from my mother, and one of the many things for which I have to bless her."[13] Hutchinson was supremely happy in this house and often said that he expected to live in it until he died.[14]

Both Charles and Frances had a gift for friendship, and in their home they served as generous hosts and warm companions. The couple's closest neighbors were among their best friends, a group which included—in addition to the Glessners—Ernest Hamill, Albert A. Sprague, Sprague's brother Otho, Adolphus Clay Bartlett and his son Frederic, and the Buckingham family and Byron L. Smith, who lived further north. Although Prairie Avenue's inhabitants were wealthy, the neighborhood had a modest small-town charm that was especially pronounced on its southern end, where the long stretch between 26th and 29th streets was not interrupted by cross streets (FIG. 8). The residents held Sunday night dinners, anniversary celebrations where the attendees sang or read poems, and luncheons with homemade favors (FIG. 9). For example, on New Year's Eve in 1900 the Hutchinsons hosted a party for twenty family members and friends, with supper in the library at 10:30 p.m. Although their guest lists were rarely very large, they often included visiting artists, scholars, and writers. These gentle gatherings stood in stark contrast to the pomp and formality of social events at the Edith Rockefeller McCormick or Potter Palmer mansions, for instance, which typically featured gold plates, towering candelabra, and servants in breeches and silk stockings. At one such affair Frances Glessner, who did not approve of ostentation, noted that the sherry glasses had been filled with whiskey by mistake.[15]

FIGURE 10. Martin A. Ryerson, the other half of the "committee of two," inherited a large fortune that his father made in the Michigan lumber trade and Chicago real estate. The partnership between Hutchinson and him was vital to the Art Institute in countless ways. Chicago History Museum, ICHi-61815.

friends of all ages with thoughtful gifts perfectly matched to the recipients—a pair of cuff buttons, a rare bottle of wine, an antique cameo, cans of special coffee that promised better sleep, and, always, great bunches of flowers. Hutchinson once sent John D. Rockefeller a package of beautiful apples. A handwritten thank-you note assured Hutchinson, "you could not have given me anything more acceptable. I eat good apples from morning until night when I can get them . . . . Apples never tasted better to me than these. I have given Mrs. Rockefeller a bite."[18] The warmth and authenticity of Hutchinson's personal relationships made many of his friends join him as staunch benefactors of both the Art Institute and the University of Chicago.

Among his connections, the bond with Martin Ryerson was central, a partnership vital to their own lives and also of great ultimate benefit to the Art Institute. Shortly after the men returned from their 1890 trip to acquire works from the Demidoff collection, Ryerson was elected a trustee, and following Henry Field's death later that year, replaced him on the executive and art committees. Although the board was always a close group bound by many business and personal ties, the importance of this extraordinary friendship was quickly recognized. Indeed, when it was time to name a negotiating team to secure the lakefront site, Hutchinson and Ryerson were unanimously appointed "a committee of two," a sobriquet that could just as easily describe their fruitful alliance over the next thirty-five years.[19]

As in many such relationships, the two men were outwardly a study in contrasts. The portly, clean-shaven Hutchinson was the kindly uncle with the cordial handshake, ready with a compliment or a folksy joke, as the occasion dictated. He liked to open talks to businessmen with the assurance that he would never "bunco" them. Ryerson, by contrast, was slender and bearded (FIG. 10). Reserved and introverted, his manner was deliberate and he projected a scholarly sensibility and quiet authority. Undoubtedly he inherited some of these traits from his parents. His father, also Martin Ryerson, who had little formal education, had spent years tramping the woods of Michigan trading furs with the Ottawa Indians, a tribe whose impassive, stoic demeanor he came to revere. He eventually entered the lumber trade in Muskegon and opened a yard in Chicago as early as 1846.

The writer Hamlin Garland's wife Zulima said about Hutchinson, "He had thousands of friends—and yet we felt (probably like hundreds of others) that our friendship was a little different."[16] He had a warm, generous personality and the capacity to make others feel understood and encouraged. Without children of his own, he was "Uncle Charley" to his nieces and nephews and a host of other young people all over town. He liked to serve up Sunday breakfasts of waffles and corned beef hash and lead wild chases around the house, winding up at St. Paul's Sunday school, where he served as superintendent for over twenty-five years.[17] As these children matured into adolescents, they found in Hutchinson a sympathetic advisor. He was always the first to hear about an engagement, a new apartment, or a change in career. He remembered

FIGURE 11. Carrie Ryerson, Martin Ryerson's wife, in the conservatory of the couple's home at 4851 Drexel Boulevard (now the Croatian Ethnic Institute). She shared her husband's aesthetic interests and served as president of the Antiquarians, an Art Institute support group, from 1908 to 1919.

After his first wife died, he married Mary Campau, a daughter of Antoine Campau, whose family had founded Grand Rapids. Martin Antoine Ryerson was born in 1856. The family moved to Europe when he was in his teens. According to John Glessner, they had intended to travel for just a year but stayed for six because Mary Ryerson so dreaded the return voyage.[20] Martin was educated in private schools in Paris and Geneva. When the family returned to Chicago in 1876, they moved into the Grand Pacific, a new luxury hotel located at Clark Street and Jackson Boulevard, and Martin went east to Harvard University, where he received a law degree in 1878. After practicing for a short time, he was put in charge of his

father's extensive lumber business while the latter managed his downtown real estate investments.[21] On Martin's twenty-fifth birthday, he married Carrie Hutchinson (FIG. 11), daughter of a wholesale hat and cap manufacturer. Coincidentally, her father, a native of Gloversville, New York, was named Charles Hutchinson. Records seem to indicate he was at most a distant relation of Benjamin Hutchinson.

When the elder Ryerson died in 1887, aside from some bequests to charity, handsome provision for his wife and a daughter from his first marriage, and small legacies to other friends and family members, the bulk of his estate—then estimated at $3,000,000 to $5,000,000—went to his son. The younger Ryerson retained some of the real estate and served on various corporate boards, including that of the Corn Exchange Bank. However, he largely used the windfall to retire from business and focus on supporting the development of his favored cultural and educational institutions. At Hutchinson's insistence, he joined the inaugural board of trustees of the University of Chicago, serving as its president from 1892 to 1922.[22] Another principal cause was the Field Museum of Natural History, where he long held the office of vice-president. He is most remembered, however, as an astute and discriminating collector who remains to this day the single most important donor in the history of the Art Institute.

What Ryerson and Hutchinson shared, beyond their common philanthropic interests and ties of affection, was a preference for a simple, clear, and methodical approach to management. Bureaucracy, with its titles, multiplication of meetings, and elaborate division of duties, was anathema to them, and this antipathy was reflected in the informal organization of the museum's early administration. Nor did either man like gaudiness or aggressive personalities, even in like-minded individuals, and this distaste was well known. On docking in New York after a European journey, they were among the passengers attempting to find their possessions in a chaotic array of parcels and baggage at the ship's warehouse. Boston artist Susan Hale appealed for their help in obtaining her belongings and later wrote to thank Hutchinson for his assistance. She realized that she had allowed Ryerson to claim a piece of silk that was probably hers but did not confront him at the time because, she wrote, "He

FIGURE 12. Interior of the Auditorium Theater, home of the Chicago Opera Company, at Michigan Avenue and Congress Street, in an illustration published in *Harper's Weekly*, December 28, 1889. Hutchinson was treasurer of the Auditorium Association and often hosted intimate suppers in the adjoining café following performances. Chicago History Museum, ICHi-61817.

thinks that strong-minded women who impose their affairs on other people are a nuisance."[23] In fact, both men avoided flamboyant characters of either sex: when the famed collector Isabella Stewart Gardner came to Chicago in early 1904 with Renaissance art authority Bernard Berenson and his wife, Mary, neither participated in the round of dinners and teas the visit inspired. They arranged for Berenson to see their collections in their absence, though Ryerson desired a detailed account of his reactions. Presumably, they also did not wish to socialize with Gardner, who held court throughout her visit in flashy gowns and diamond headdresses, her conversation studded with witty barbs and innuendo prompted by her jealousy of the attention lavished on Berenson. Her visit was partly motivated by a desire to promote her protégé George Proctor, a young pianist scheduled for a solo performance with the Theodore Thomas Orchestra,

predecessor of the present Chicago Symphony Orchestra. She had hoped to enlist Hutchinson's help in securing further engagements for Proctor but quickly discerned there was no reason to pursue the matter. Sensing his utter lack of interest, Gardner wrote her friend Frances Glessner, "I know him so little that I fear he might not like it."[24]

Hutchinson and Ryerson were close in age, their wives got along well, and both couples were childless, so their social lives meshed easily. They shared dinners and evenings of music or theater. Devoted opera lovers, the Ryersons reserved a box for opening nights and held regular seats for every event so they would never miss a performance (FIG. 12). In autumn and spring the men would take fishing expeditions, traveling by private railcar to Sandusky, Ohio, where they boarded a steamer bound for the Pelee Club, a rustic camp on an island in the Canadian side of Lake Erie

FIGURE 13. Exterior view of the Pelee Club, 1883/89. Hutchinson was a member of this rustic fishing retreat on a Canadian island in Lake Erie. Organized in 1883, the club had a roster that included many notable Chicagoans, among them Ryerson, Marshall Field, Robert Todd Lincoln, and George M. Pullman. Pelee Club Archives.

(FIG. 13). The members of this club, mostly captains of the Midwest's largest industries, enjoyed the opportunity to relax in a backwoods atmosphere of gravel roads and simple food, near waters where bass and walleye pike were plentiful. True to character, whenever Hutchinson reeled in a large catch, he sent generous packets to friends back home. These restful outings also boosted Ryerson's fragile constitution. Suffering frequent bouts of ill health, he wintered for some years in Augusta, Palm Beach, and Savannah. In 1895 the Hutchinsons and Ryersons bought ninety adjoining acres on Strawberry Hill in North Carolina's Blue Ridge Mountains, directly across from Biltmore, George Vanderbilt's recently completed French Renaissance château. Enamored of the clear bracing air and forested countryside, they made plans to build winter homes there and attract a small colony of Chicago friends to join them. By March 1897 Ryerson had approved a set of blueprints and construction was set to begin. That same year, however, he rented Bonnie Brae, an estate in Lake Geneva, Wisconsin. He so loved the property that the North Carolina plan was abandoned, Bonnie Brae purchased and remodeled, and a sizable dock installed for a sleek new yacht that was ready the following summer. Soon after, the Hutchinsons also bought land nearby, acquiring a long wooded stretch of lakefront on which they built a large half-timber house they called Wychwood (FIG. 14). Here Hutchinson at last found the setting where he could fully pursue his growing love of botany. With advice from Charles Sprague Sargent, director of the Arnold Arboretum at Harvard University and America's leading horticulturalist, and under the full-time care of William Longland, a talented local gardener, the property was developed as a bird sanctuary and nature preserve, with lush forests and winding paths banked by thousands of species of indigenous shrubs and wildflowers.[25]

* * *

It was on their annual journeys abroad that Hutchinson and Ryerson shared their deepest connection as friends and fellow connoisseurs. Their travels took them far afield, exposing them to the art of past civilizations and exotic present-day cultures (FIG. 1). These experiences engendered in them a cosmopolitan perspective and largeness of spirit with which they enriched their Chicago milieu. What had begun as scouting trips for the museum and voyages of recuperation evolved into a way of life the pair found very satisfying, one that other men and women of the leisure class undoubtedly wished to emulate.

The Ryersons usually left in late autumn, sometimes stopping in Florida before sailing to Europe ahead of the Hutchinsons, who celebrated the holidays in Chicago. (Charles never wanted to miss the rollicking Thanksgiving at Hull House, where he provided—and carved—the turkeys, or the Apollo Club's Christmas Day performance of Handel's *Messiah*.) Sometime in early winter, the two couples would meet at a favorite hotel and embark on their joint itinerary. Over the course of two dozen years, they visited most of the capitals of Europe, viewing its cultural landmarks—cathedrals, monuments, palaces, ruins, and always a multitude of galleries and museums. They took

FIGURE 14. In 1901 the Hutchinsons bought property on Lake Geneva in Wisconsin and built this half-timbered, Elizabethan-style country house they called Wychwood.

unhurried excursions to the forest of Fontainebleau, the villas of Florence, and the cottage gardens of England. In 1909 Frances Hutchinson published *Motoring in the Balkans*, a sprightly account of a two-month auto journey from Trieste to Vienna, illustrated by over one hundred of her own snapshots (FIG. 15).[26] The tale contains descriptions of Diocletian's palace in Croatia, secluded mountain cloisters, and colorful village markets, but it is also part road comedy, telling how the dignified but game travelers coped with punctured tires, incomprehensible foreign dialects, and goats who refused to move out of the path. For some years Hutchinson kept a simple travel log of his own, and it was always the small incidents that stood out in his memory—a sudden rain shower in the Azores, when he took shelter under a banyan tree, or a glimpse of the king of Spain and his court standing in full regalia on a train platform. He reveled in the Gothic quadrangles of Oxford and loved to tell the story of the time he enjoyed a full English breakfast at Cambridge, at which

the master of Trinity College himself placed a pat of butter at every guest's plate, a traditional gesture of welcome.[27]

Hutchinson made friends easily. Years later, he would sometimes receive letters from strangers he had briefly met on cruises or in train compartments who fondly remembered the encounter. Additionally, he could overlook boorish behavior in the presence of great talent. Having met James McNeill Whistler in Paris, he recalled, "His artistic genius and brilliant personality made one always regret the lack of affable, gentlemanly manners in which he was notoriously deficient." Yet Hutchinson described their interview as "entirely agreeable."[28] Ryerson, by contrast, was not nearly so flexible and seems to have saved most of his enthusiasm for the goods in antique stores and auction rooms. A reporter published an account of a light-hearted encounter with Ryerson in Paris, "when in his quiet way he was feeling like the whole Sox team, and all over a cracked old platter."[29] But surely he dropped a bit of this natural reserve when he and Hutchinson attended the Folies Bergère and must have relaxed slightly when in places familiar to him from his European childhood. Indeed, in the right setting, Ryerson could even show a sense of play and a sly wit. Once, while aboard ship in the Mediterranean, he found himself dining next to Robert Morss Lovett, an assistant professor of English at the University of Chicago. Lovett ordered what he thought to be a fine bottle of wine. Wincing, Ryerson removed the wine card from Lovett's hand and pointed to a vintage Riesling instead. As Lovett told it, Ryerson, whose acute discrimination extended across many fields, thereafter supervised the choice of wine, permitting himself, "against doctor's orders, a small sip of each new bottle to validate the selection." Lovett proposed that the university sponsor a course in wine tasting, with the students spending four successive summers sampling the cellars of Europe, taking advantage of the hospitality of the growers. Intrigued, Ryerson began working out the details on paper. But when Lovett rhapsodized that such a course might even constitute a prerequisite for initiation into "the higher criticism," he said, "Mr. Ryerson suspected satire and closed up."[30]

In 1900 Hutchinson and Ryerson visited Russia with William Rainey Harper (FIG. 16), president of the University of Chicago, and the philanthropist Charles R. Crane, who wished to endow a chair in Russian art, history, and literature on condition that it be taught by visiting Slavic scholars of the highest caliber.[31] Their tour included a brief stay in Moscow and several visits to the art collections of the Hermitage in St. Petersburg. The party was also privileged to spend an evening with Leo Tolstoy, who transfixed them with his fervor on behalf of the Boers in the war then raging in Africa. Hutchinson came away convinced that Tolstoy was "not merely a Russian writer. He is a world writer." But Hutchinson and Ryerson agreed that the highlight of their life abroad was a remarkable visit with Czar Nicholas II at Tsarkoe-Selo, the country estate of the Russian imperial family. On the appointed day, the four men, in dress suits, tall hats, and white gloves, were driven in two carriages to the estate's Neoclassical Alexander Palace, where a liveried servant guided them through a maze of gilded staterooms. Passing into a library filled with books in many languages, they were then led down a long hall to yet another reception

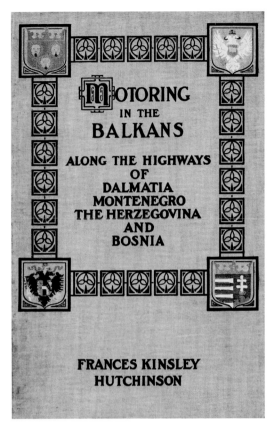

FIGURE 15. Frances Hutchinson's book *Motoring in the Balkans* (1909), with a cover designed by students in Louis J. Millet's class at the School of the Art Institute. Charles Hutchinson offered the group a cash prize for a successful design. Ryerson and Burnham Libraries, Art Institute of Chicago.

room. There they waited until precisely twelve o'clock, when they were invited into the private cabinet of the czar, a room Hutchinson recalled as "beautiful and home-like, with many modern pictures on the wall." The twenty-nine-year-old ruler was clad simply in a Russian colonel's uniform—white duck jacket, dark trousers, and leather boots. He shook hands with each man, spoke fluent English, and impressed the visitors deeply with his frank and thoughtful manner and earnest desire to advance educational opportunities for the mass of poor Russians as well as aspiring students in the United States. He also promised to help find suitable professors for their project, and true to his pledge, in time several accomplished scholars arrived on campus, including Thomas G. Masaryk, who later became the founder and first president of Czechoslovakia.

FIGURE 16. William Rainey Harper, first president of the University of Chicago. In the last letter he wrote Hutchinson before his premature death from cancer in 1906, he urged him to "keep an eye wide open for the great interests here at the University." Chicago History Museum, ICHi-31031. Photograph by Blakaleer.

Another unusual adventure was the Hutchinsons' and Ryersons' expedition just a few years earlier to British India and the Far East. Sailing through the Suez Canal and down the Red Sea, they began their odyssey in Colombo and proceeded to visit Bombay, Ajmere, Agra, Lahore, and Calcutta, spending a few weeks in the Lower Himalayas at Darjeeling, then a hill station where the British colonials went to escape the heat of Indian summers. Accommodations were extremely basic. Hutchinson reported to friends back home that the two couples were obliged to carry bedding and towels everywhere as neither the hotels nor trains furnished them. "The best of all food here," he added, "is generally to be found at the railway stations."[32] These challenges did not hinder their enjoyment of the temples of southern India and the rich Mughal heritage of the north, with its mix of ancient mosques, walled gardens, and recent Victorian architecture. Martin Ryerson perceptively observed that it was wrong to think of India as one nation, that it was "more like a great continent containing many countries" and that "nowhere is this more apparent than in the arts."[33] Moving east through Burma and Hong Kong, they ended their trip in Japan (FIG. 17). As the group traveled, they made many purchases—cashmere jackets and shawls, emeralds and pearls, embroideries, enamelware, and silks. The

Hutchinsons stayed two weeks in Japan, but the Ryersons remained a month or more. It is likely that on this visit Martin first purchased some of the brocade robes, eighteenth-century pottery, and hand-illustrated manuscripts and books that he presented to the museum many years later. Correspondence with a few dealers indicates that the Hutchinsons expressed interest in "very old and rare collections," but it appears that the bowls, lacquer boxes, and vases they ultimately bought were mostly handsome curios.

It was Egypt that most captured Hutchinson's imagination and rekindled his romance with ancient civilizations born in George Howland's classes at the Chicago High School. The Hutchinsons and Ryersons made three trips to Egypt—in 1892, 1894, and 1910. Sailing up the Nile on a low-slung houseboat (or *dahabeah*), their progress slowed or hurried by prevailing winds, they could never calculate in the morning where they might be at night. In 1894 they were on the water for seventy days, which provided ample opportunity to view pyramids, ruined tombs, and temples (FIG. 18). Hutchinson rhapsodized about "this land of yesterday," full of marvels whose magnificence could not be adequately conveyed in words. He was awestruck by the colossal statues of Abu Simbel and rode seventeen miles on the back of a donkey to see the Valley of the Kings. He was enchanted by sunsets that seemed to flood the sky, the singing of the Nubian rowers, and the muezzins' calls urging high and low to prayer. He immediately and instinctively recognized the need to protect the rapidly deteriorating monuments from the ravages of weather and vandalism. The Arabic custom of appropriating eighth- and ninth-century tombstones for new burials, defacing the inscriptions in the process, disturbed him as well. "Five or ten years will be sufficient to blot out all traces of these . . . valuable records," he wrote to Harper. "A small sum would preserve them."[34]

The late nineteenth and early twentieth centuries were years of prodigious archaeological exploration, when representatives of American and European museums, whose subscriptions covered much of the cost of these digs, vied heatedly for their share of the finds uncovered every day at a multitude of sites. The Art Institute was an accredited subscriber, but Hutchinson and Ryerson also came armed with letters of introduction to key members of the archaeology

FIGURE 17. The Hutchinsons and the Ryersons in rickshaws in Japan, 1896.

community who could lead them to responsible agents and dealers. One contact was the Reverend Chauncey Murch, a Presbyterian missionary, experienced amateur Egyptologist, and knowledgeable collector. Another was Archibald Sayce, an Oxford professor and pioneer Assyriologist. These two men, and some other scholars the Chicagoans met en route, helped them acquire many objects of great merit, including bronze statuettes, delicate gold and glass jewelry, kohl and ointment jars, papyrus specimens, stone vessels, tablets, and terracotta items.[35] Indeed, the treasures Hutchinson brought home from Egypt are among his most important gifts to the museum and remain at the core of its ancient art collection (FIGS. 20-21). A few other Art Institute supporters shared in the cost of these purchases, most prominently Henry H. Getty, a fellow trustee. Getty, who had been a business partner of Ryerson's father, was then retired and living with his daughter

Alice in an elegant apartment on the Champs Elysées. Both father and daughter were erudite connoisseurs, and after Ryerson gave funds to construct a museum library in 1902, Getty sent annual gifts of valuable books, catalogues, guides, maps, and long runs of European journals that the library could not otherwise afford. In 1894 Murch loaned a portion of his antiquities collection to the Art Institute, and Hutchinson and Getty purchased some pieces, including a group of commemorative scarabs, at the close of the exhibition.

Hutchinson acquired more objects for the museum on his last trip to Egypt in 1910. By that time the Aswan Dam had been built; this project benefited the region economically but put its archaeological treasures at greater risk. Cairo had modernized substantially. Although Hutchinson was glad to note that, "the terrace of Shepheard's Hotel is still the most cosmopolitan spot on the face of the earth," there were many

FIGURE 18. The Hutchinsons and Ryersons made three visits to Egypt. An enthusiastic amateur photographer, Frances Hutchinson used her ever-present Kodak to take many snapshots of the ruins they saw there. Charles L. Hutchinson Papers, The Newberry Library, Chicago.

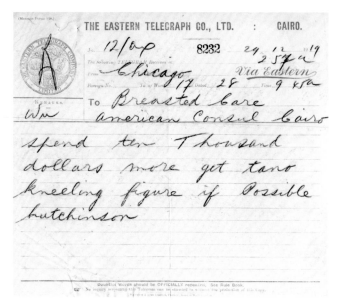

FIGURE 19. An urgent cable from Hutchinson to James Henry Breasted in Cairo, confirming William French's observation that Hutchinson was always "ready for anything good." Breasted was named the Art Institute's honorary curator of Egyptian antiquities in 1920. Courtesy of Oriental Institute Museum.

more tourists, the streets were crowded with automobiles, and the first steamboat to sail the Nile had been dismantled and transformed into a dockside café.[36] Instead of the slow-going *dahabeah*, the Hutchinsons and Ryersons chartered a steamer, and their trek to the Valley of the Kings was made in sand carts, a comfortable as well as time-saving method of transportation. On returning home, the display and care of their newly acquired relics was entrusted not to the museum's still-minimal staff but to James Henry Breasted, a University of Chicago professor already established as America's foremost authority on the Near East (FIG. 19).

* * *

Throughout the period leading up to World War I, Hutchinson and Ryerson continued to act on behalf of the Art Institute in the art markets of Paris, London, and New York. Much was available for purchase, but misattributions and outright fakes abounded, and prices for works of every style and period were rapidly increasing, buoyed by demand from the millionaires of America's Gilded Age. Competition

was keen among the East Coast museums, and accomplishing major acquisitions required ingenuity even for those institutions with ample endowments. The Metropolitan Museum, enriched by a series of gifts and bequests, was assembling one of the premier collections in the world. By contrast, the Art Institute, still struggling to find donors for the Demidoff purchase and saddled with perpetual deficits, was virtually stymied. Wealthy Chicagoans were generous, but tended to direct their donations to hospitals, institutions for the needy, and universities. After the city transferred control of the lakefront to the newly created South Park Board and levied a half-mill property tax for the support of its land and buildings, the museum began to receive about $50,000 a year for operating expenses. This income provided some measure of budget relief, but the trustees were of necessity a prudent group, reluctant to assume undue risk. Thus the galleries continued to be hung chiefly with special exhibitions and shows of loans from private individuals (which admittedly included some spectacular works). It was not until the early 1920s, beginning with the Palmer and Kimball bequests, that a permanent collection of real substance began to take form.

Still, even in the lean years, the esteemed "committee of two" was able to make some wonderful acquisitions. They cultivated cordial relations with a roster of dealers, including Durand-Ruel, Ehrichs, Fischer, Georges Petit, Knoedler, Macbeth, and Reinhardt, and William French assured all his colleagues that "Mr. Hutchinson and Mr. Ryerson are ready for anything good."[37] Every so often, the two men would locate an exceptional object, send it back to Chicago, and hope that a donor would sooner or later come forward to cover the cost. Supposedly, in 1900 they were eating breakfast in Paris when they spotted a newspaper announcement of a sale at the Château de Méréville, noted for its picturesque, folly-filled gardens designed by Hubert Robert, or "Robert des Ruines," the eighteenth century landscape painter. As quickly as possible, they traveled to the auction, where they were able to snare the four large panels Robert painted for the château's dining room before representatives from the Louvre obtained the authority to increase their bid.[38] These works depicting scenes from antiquity were subsequently funded by Richard T. Crane, Adolphus Clay Bartlett, William C. Hibbard, and Clarence Buckingham. That same year, James McNeill Whistler's *Nocturne: Blue and Gold—Southampton Water*, an oil signed with the painter's butterfly mark, entered the collection (FIG. 22). Henri Fantin-Latour's portrait of Édouard Manet was acquired in 1905 (FIG. 23). In 1909, partly thanks to Buckingham's great friendship with the New York scholar and Metropolitan Museum of Art trustee Howard Mansfield, the Art Institute bought Mansfield's collection of rare Charles Meryon etchings for the impressive sum of $30,000. The Whistler, Fantin-Latour, and Meryon purchases were made possible through the 1898 bequest from Elizabeth Hammond Stickney, one of the Chicago Academy of Design's early trustees.[39] Manet's important canvas *The Philosopher* was acquired in 1910 and exemplifies Hutchinson's deliberate and patient approach to obtaining funding. A. A. Munger, heir to a grain elevator fortune, had died in 1898, leaving the museum a large collection of paintings (including William Bouguereau's popular *The Bathers*). His substantial fortune, however, went largely to cousins, including Alexander A. McKay. When McKay died in 1914, his will left $100,000 to the museum for "the maintenance and enlargement of the Munger collection."[40] One of very few major

FIGURE 20. Egyptian. *Statuette of Re Horakhty*, Third Intermediate Period, Dynasty 21–25 (c. 1069–656 B.C.). Bronze with gilt; 25 x 8.3 x 10.5 cm (9 7/8 x 3 1/4 x 4 1/8 in.). Gift of Henry H. Getty, Charles L. Hutchinson, and Robert H. Fleming, 1894. 261.

bequests in this period, the gift was cause for great jubilation. It covered not only the Manet (which was added to the Munger collection in 1918 at Hutchinson's suggestion) but many subsequent purchases, including significant works by Théodore Gericault, Luca Cambiaso, Sir Joshua Reynolds, and the extraordinary *Landscape with Saint John on Patmos* by Nicolas Poussin.

Nevertheless, the two self-appointed scouts were continually frustrated by the trustees' excessive caution. In 1909 Ryerson suggested acquiring a picture by Johan Barthold Jongkind, the Dutch landscape painter and contemporary of the Impressionists. The art committee turned it down. A few years later he proposed a vivid portrait by Francisco

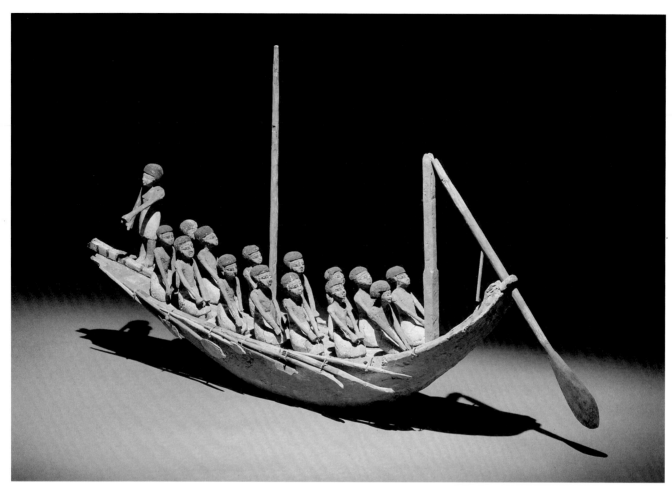

FIGURE 21. Egyptian. *Model Boat*, Middle Kingdom, Dynasty 11/12 (c. 2046–1794 B.C.). Wood with pigment; 61 x 104 x 23 cm (24 x 41 x 9 in.). Gift of Henry H. Getty, Charles L. Hutchinson, Robert H. Fleming, and Norman W. Harris, 1894.241.

de Goya, with the same result. In February 1909, Hutchinson requested that Durand-Ruel send a Mary Cassatt painting of a woman and child to Chicago. It hung in the Trustees Room, its fate undetermined until the following October, when Ryerson finally declared that if the museum would not take the painting, he would buy it himself. Hutchinson diplomatically asked if the museum might show it in the annual exhibition of American art, thus giving the board a little more time to become accustomed to it. By December Durand-Ruel had offered to send four more Cassatt pictures for consideration. In January two of these arrived, including a canvas titled *The Child's Bath*. At the end of January, just before Hutchinson left for Egypt, this last pic-

ture was finally purchased and the others returned, despite the resolute indifference of French, who could say only, "I am rather surprised at the influence of Miss Cassatt over our people . . . . Her work appears to me very extreme."⁴¹ Such recalcitrance undoubtedly inspired Hutchinson to suggest the formation of a new support group, the Friends of American Art, composed of individuals who agreed to contribute $200 a year for five years toward the purchase of American art. By mid-summer its roster had grown to 142 members. In a few years, this successful organization's many acquisitions included George Bellows's *Love of Winter*; John Singer Sargent's *The Fountain, Villa Torlonia, Frascati*, and *Mrs. Charles Dyer Gifford*; Gilbert Stuart's portrait of General Dearborn, and Whistler's *The Artist in His Studio*.

Indisputably, the accomplishment that secured the importance of the Hutchinson-Ryerson partnership for all time was obtaining El Greco's masterpiece *The Assumption of the Virgin* (FIG. 25). The acquisition was a triumph of courage, judgment, and perseverance—a coup in the marketplace and a victory of persuasion at home. The course of this purchase was so unlikely that it might never have happened at all. In 1901 Cassatt, who was advising the American collectors Horace and Louisine Havemeyer, developed a passion for the paintings of Goya and El Greco. With the help of the dealer Joseph Wicht, she searched for examples of the artists' work hidden away in the parlors and closets of the Spanish aristocracy. With his superb connections in Madrid, Wicht managed to have even long-sealed cases opened, and according to Cassatt in one of these they discovered *The Assumption of the Virgin*, commissioned in 1577 as the altarpiece of Santo Domingo el Antiguo in Toledo.[42] It is a powerfully expressive composition showing the Virgin ascending to heaven, high above an empty tomb surrounded by astonished apostles. Cassatt wrote Louisine Havemeyer, "It is perfectly splendid in color; I think it must be an early work for it is so Venetian in style and composition."[43] In the nineteenth century, the clergy had replaced the original painting with a copy and sold El Greco's canvas to a member of the Bourbon family.

Over thirteen feet high and seven feet wide, it seemed too large for a domestic setting, and the Havemeyers bought El Greco's *Portrait of a Cardinal* instead. After the death of the owner's widow in 1902, *The Assumption of the Virgin* hung in the Museo de Prado for two years until Durand-Ruel, with the help of a loan from the Havemeyers, pried it away from the family for the sum of 100,000 francs (or about $1,700). The Havemeyers offered to sell the painting to the Metropolitan Museum at the price of the loan but were informed by a trustee that the institution had just secured "a finer one."[44] Cassatt and Durand-Ruel than approached the Philadelphia Academy of the Fine Arts, but they were turned away. Likewise, the Museum of Fine Arts in Boston expressed no interest. On the advice of John Singer Sargent, they had recently purchased an El Greco and in any case were in the midst of plans for a new building.

As early as February 1904, Cassatt had written to her friend Grace Gassette, a Chicago artist then living in Paris, "I wish Mr. Hutchinson could manage to have for the Chicago Museum a work that I know of to be had in Spain. He seems to be the only man that is intelligently working for a public gallery in America."[45] On April 12, 1904, the day before he departed for home, Hutchinson did visit Cassatt, and it seems likely that he first discussed the painting with her that afternoon. However, it was not until the institutions mentioned above had rejected it that Cassatt began to court the Art Institute in earnest. In January 1905, she wrote Hutchinson, "I think you cannot fail to be struck with the Greco . . . . I doubt if such another is for sale in Europe," and noted its perfect, untouched condition.[46] Hutchinson and Ryerson probably viewed the painting in Paris that winter. Its $40,000 price tag must have given them pause, because it was not until January 1906 that Durand-Ruel notified French that the canvas had arrived in New York and would be shipped out on consignment the following week. In Chicago it was hung on the north wall of the central gallery and, with Durand-Ruel's permission, left uncovered at least part of the time. Local and national art critics were quick with negative judgments. At that time El Greco was still an obscure figure almost unknown in the United States, and viewers who did see his work were often puzzled or repelled by his typically elongated figures, which seemed to them distorted and crude. Some news accounts contained factual errors, and reporters who had not even seen the painting complained of its unfinished appearance and "ashy" colors. Among the trustees in town that month there was little or no comment. Charles Deering was its only fervent supporter. As directed, French went east to view El Greco canvases in Boston, Cleveland, and New York. While writing Hutchinson that none of these works compared with *The Assumption of the Virgin*, he privately expressed to others his preference for using the money to pay off debt.[47] In Europe Hutchinson and Ryerson saw more of the artist's work at the Prado and drove to Toledo to see the church where the painting had hung. Hutchinson wired repeatedly that he had asked Durand-Ruel for more time. In May, after he returned home, the art committee voted to recommend the purchase of the painting. In June, seven trustees supported the acquisition, six were opposed,

FIGURE 22. James McNeill Whistler (American, 1843–1903). *Nocturne: Blue and Gold—Southampton Water*, 1872. Oil on canvas; 50.5 x 76 cm (19 ⅞ x 29 ¹⁵⁄₁₆ in.). Stickney Fund, 1900.52.

and eight had still to decide. During that month Hutchinson and Ryerson must surely have lobbied the board vigorously, appealing to each member's highest aspirations for the museum, for in July the trustees voted unanimously to buy the painting.

The Assumption of the Virgin went on permanent display in October 1907, suitably showcased in a brilliant gold Spanish Renaissance–inspired frame designed by the Boston artist Hermann Dudley Murphy (FIG. 24). It was not funded until 1915, when Hutchinson persuaded his old Prairie Avenue neighbor Nancy Atwood Sprague to present it as a memorial to her recently deceased husband. In the following years the painting came to be celebrated as the Art Institute's signal masterpiece, and it is still considered El Greco's greatest work outside Spain. An interesting coda to the saga of its

acquisition comes from French's account of a visit he made in 1909 to Archer M. Huntington, stepson of the railway magnate Collis Huntington and a major art collector as well as the founder of the Hispanic Society of America. The Art Institute wished to arrange an exhibition of Joaquín Sorolla's work, some of which was then on display at the Hispanic Society in New York. The eccentric Huntington summoned French to his house on Fifth Avenue at midnight. In the course of their conversation, Huntington told French that while *The Assumption of the Virgin* was still in the hands of the Bourbon family it had been offered to him at a price of $15,000, but at that time he had been unable to go see it. "Otherwise," French reported to Hutchinson, "he says, we never would have got it."[48]

FIGURE 23. Henri Fantin-Latour (French, 1836–1904). *Édouard Manet*, 1867. Oil on canvas; 117.5 x 90 cm (46 ¼ x 35 ⁷⁄₁₆ in.). Stickney Fund, 1905.207. In spring 1904, Hutchinson had this painting sent from the dealer Durand-Ruel for consideration by the museum's art committee. It excited great interest and was acquired comparatively quickly.

FIGURE 24. Installation view of El Greco's *The Assumption of the Virgin*, c. 1917. The frame, designed by Hermann Dudley Murphy of Boston, has since been replaced.

FIGURE 25. El Greco (Domenikos Theotokopoulos) (Spanish, born Crete, 1541–1614). *The Assumption of the Virgin*, 1577–79. Oil on canvas; 403.2 x 211.8 cm (158 ¾ x 83 ¾ in.). Gift of Nancy Atwood Sprague in memory of Albert Arnold Sprague, 1906.99.

"THE CONSTANT IMPROVER"

BOTH HUTCHINSON AND RYERSON devoted much of their lives to the creation of a great museum, but over time the focus of their energies diverged. After 1910 Ryerson, having carefully assembled a small private collection of exceptional quality, increasingly concentrated on making acquisitions for himself. In 1912 he wrote from New York, "I have seen so many pictures here that I am dizzy."[1] He bought works by Goya, Homer, Sargent, Edgar Degas, Auguste Renoir, and more of the early Dutch, French, and Italian masters who had intrigued him from the start. Many of these paintings were immediately displayed in the museum's galleries, and the entire collection (which grew even larger and more diverse) was eventually bequeathed to the Art Institute—perhaps the single most important gift the museum received in the twentieth century.[2]

While Hutchinson continued to collect for a time, albeit on a more modest scale, he gradually emerged as the quintessential public man.[3] Active across a wide range of civic and municipal organizations, he was most visible as the face of the Art Institute on the local and national stages, and used his renown to help various arts organizations. He served as an advisor for the American fine arts department at the 1900 Exposition universelle in Paris, and together with Ryerson and Charles Deering, rounded up loans for a Chicago room in the Palace of Fine Arts at the 1904 Louisiana Purchase

Exposition in St. Louis. He was among the first to rouse support for his good friend Daniel Burnham's campaign for the City Beautiful, which sought to make better use of Chicago's lakefront site and create a system of parks and boulevards to rival the great urban spaces of Europe. Highly respected in national museum circles, Hutchinson was an officer of the Germanic Museum Association (now the Busch-Reisinger Museum) in Cambridge, Massachusetts, and of the National Academy of Art in Washington, D. C., where he served as its first vice-president under J. Pierpont Morgan. Through an inspired speech and a series of meetings with donors, he helped raise the funds necessary to build the Minneapolis Institute of Arts, where he was elected a trustee in 1914. Similarly, at the opening of the Toledo Museum of Art, which was packed with supporters from Chicago, its founder Edward Drummond Libbey declared the organization "a child of the Art Institute." Hutchinson's influence extended even to the Metropolitan Museum of Art through his close friendship with its president, Robert W. De Forest. Elected an honorary life fellow of the Metropolitan, he gave a major address at its fiftieth anniversary celebration in 1920. Thus it is not surprising that when Elihu Root, as Theodore Roosevelt's secretary of state, organized the American Federation of Arts (essentially an early federal bureau of fine arts), he asked Hutchinson to serve as its first president. In recognition of these many efforts on behalf of the arts and humanities in America, Harvard University awarded Hutchinson an honorary master of arts degree in 1915, a tribute even this modest man confessed to accepting with enormous pride.[4]

Throughout his career, Hutchinson also capitalized on his reputation to benefit the Art Institute. In spite of the chronic struggle to raise operating funds and assemble a

FIGURE 1. Installation view of the International Exhibition of Modern Art (the Armory Show) as it appeared at the Art Institute of Chicago. Many paintings by Henri Matisse were on display, including, from right to left, *The Red Studio* (1911; Museum of Modern Art, New York), *Le Luxe II* (1907–08; Statens Museum for Kunst, Copenhagen), *Girl with a Black Cat* (1910; private collection), *Young Sailor II* (1906; Metropolitan Museum of Art, New York), and *Joaquina* (1911; Národni Galerie, Prague). Pierre Bonnard's *Provençal Conversation* (1912/13; Národni Galerie, Prague) is visible at the center of the wall on the left. The large sculpture at right is *Woman Kneeling* by Wilhelm Lembruck.

FIGURE 2. View from the south of Blackstone Hall, c. 1905. This space displayed the museum's plaster cast collection. The large arched doorway at the right is a cast of a portal from the church of Notre Dame du Port in Clermont-Ferrand, Auvergne, France.

of the Great Lakes, installed on the museum's South Terrace in 1913 to much acclaim (FIG. 3).[5]

As in everything else, Hutchinson dominated the internal administration of the museum. Seated at his double partners desk almost every morning, he was the acknowledged "prime mover" in policy matters both big and small.[6] Chiefly concerned with creating a large and diverse constituency of museumgoers, he was obsessed with attendance figures and sometimes stood beside the guard at the door as each entrant was "clicked in" on a small thumb press. It was a matter of great pride to him that the Art Institute received more visitors than each of the eastern museums, including the mighty Metropolitan. Hutchinson insisted that most exhibition catalogues be simply produced so they could be distributed to the public for free or at a modest cost, and in 1907 he introduced the *Bulletin of the Art Institute of Chicago* as another educational tool. At first a quarterly, the journal was soon published several times a year with longer articles and more announcements. Hutchinson pushed for a full lecture calendar of popular speakers, sometimes with the ironic result that people who could not get into the overcrowded hall threatened to resign their memberships. Moreover, just as he was accustomed to decorating his own home, at the museum he liked to choose the wall colors and floor coverings in the galleries, the finishes on cases, and the heights of pedestals. He even attended to object labels and requested frequent reinstallations. As French noted, "Mr. Hutchinson . . . likes to see things in a new light."[7] His instincts about exhibition design were very good: he often advised artists fortunate enough to have solo shows that they ought to display only half the items, so as to highlight their strongest work. He was especially pleased when visitors to exhibitions of paintings by Chicago artists (where most of the canvases were for sale) asked for his help in choosing a picture. He liked to say that no living person knew more about the Art Institute than he did, having served so long "as its President (and Janitor for I have often found the term synonymous)."[8]

worthy collection, he—always "a bricks and mortar man"—pushed continually to realize the architects' original design and enlarge the museum even further to accommodate its growing roster of activities. His personal friendships attracted gifts to erect such spaces as Fullerton and Blackstone halls (FIG. 2), and his election to the South Park Board Commission in 1907 eased many potential legal problems among the Art Institute, the city, and the Illinois Central Railroad. By 1910 the central part of the museum's building was finished and the galleries were fitted with mosaic and marble. Although enough money never materialized to construct the planned central dome, the installation of the grand staircase was an exhilarating moment. Another friend, pioneer lumber magnate Benjamin F. Ferguson, observed on his travels abroad that the charm of European cities was enhanced by the impressive statues and fountains in their parks and boulevards. Accordingly, when he died in 1905, he endowed a fund to be administered by the Art Institute to embellish Chicago in a similar fashion. Hutchinson chaired the Ferguson Fund, and its inaugural sculpture was Lorado Taft's graceful *Fountain*

* * *

Many talented individuals worked under Hutchinson's at times overpowering influence. French was director for thirty years, and Newton H. Carpenter (FIG. 4) was business manager and effective superintendent of buildings and grounds for thirty-four. The museum staff remained small and necessarily versatile. Bessie Bennett was the only full-time curator, in charge of textiles and decorative arts.[9] A number of trained librarians, a registrar, various assistants, a crew of installers, and guards were the only other regular employees. Among those hired on an as-needed basis were Alfred Emerson, a Classics scholar who wrote general catalogues about the museum's collection and worked specifically with its ancient art. Professor S. Cho-Yo, who had come to Chicago as director of Japanese fine art at the World's Columbian Exposition, was often asked to evaluate Asian works, and F. H. C. Sammons, an unassuming Englishman, was hired to repair and conserve pictures. Otherwise, most expertise was provided by a variety of visiting artists, dealers, scholars, and specialists from other museums when necessary.

French managed his responsibilities, often performed under great pressure, with tact, sympathy, and humor. He was protective of his small staff, maintained warm relationships with most of his colleagues in the field, and if he eventually grew a bit jaded ("The usual widow has just called with a famous Rembrandt"), he was always loyal to the Art Institute.[10] His greatest love seems to have been reserved for the school, which he continued to lead during his entire tenure (FIG. 5). He was proud of the fact that, except for the space it occupied, which belonged to the museum, the school was self-supporting. When Chicago's board of education granted public school teachers credit for some of its classes, he was overjoyed to welcome over one thousand of them to the school's evening and Saturday sessions. He realized early on, however, that Hutchinson was far more interested in the museum, and there is something plaintive in his confession, "I always wished the Art Institute was named the Chicago Museum and School of Art."[11] An entertaining lecturer himself, he gave his faculty the freedom to teach as they thought best and did not distinguish between the fine and applied arts. He called himself a suffragist and refused to segregate

FIGURE 3. Lorado Taft's *Fountain of the Great Lakes*, 1907–13. Originally installed along the Art Institute's South Terrace (as shown in this c. 1915 postcard), it was the first sculpture commissioned by the Ferguson Fund, established to beautify the parks and boulevards of Chicago. In 1965 it was relocated to the museum's South Stanley McCormick Memorial Court. Collection of Celia Hilliard.

classes, exhibitions, and prizes by gender (FIG. 6). He was especially proud of his wife, an accomplished portrait and landscape painter whose work was held by some museums. "I have always believed," he told friends, "she could paint as well as Mrs. MacMonnies, Miss Cassatt, Miss Beaux and the rest."[12]

French never claimed a broad critical understanding of art. By his own admission, his taste was guided by classical principles of composition, beauty of form, and elevation of

FIGURE 4. Newton H. Carpenter, the Art Institute's secretary and business manager. An indefatigable promoter, he was in his element planning for the Armory Show. French reported he was "working it up as a kind of circus and sensation."

FIGURE 5. William French conducting a "chalk talk" in which he illustrated the principles of art with freehand sketches made at the podium. His most popular lecture was titled "The Wit and Wisdom of the Crayon."

subject. For at least twenty years, the centerpiece of the museum's exhibition calendar was the annual autumn show of American work, most of it assembled by Sara Hallowell, the Art Institute's agent in Paris. Her astute judgment and extensive connections enabled her to secure the best paintings by Americans working abroad. French supplemented her choices with canvases from around the country, often benefiting from the professional ties of his brother, the sculptor Daniel Chester French. The winter season included shows of work by Chicago artists as well as special exhibitions of varying degrees of significance.

However, this comfortable and longstanding arrangement began to teeter with the emergence of the modernist avant-garde, which departed dramatically from previous standards of beauty and composition. Concurrently, more and more people came to believe that museums ought to be not only repositories for acknowledged masterpieces but

also showcases for new artistic developments. As early as 1907, Ryerson suggested to French, "We ought to enlarge our range."[13] The eclectic Hutchinson, who would go on to sponsor the Little Theater movement in Chicago and Harriet Monroe's modernist magazine, *Poetry*, was always open to whatever fresh ideas might keep the Art Institute at the forefront of cultural life.[14] At this point the board of trustees and the museum's public needed, if not a passionate advocate of the avant-garde, then at least an intelligent guide to these new movements, someone who could interpret them to a curious audience. As director, French was the logical person to step into this role. However, he was himself mystified by these developments and had nothing to offer. It may have been that years of deference and the lack of much real authority had dampened his spirit and sense of initiative. As energetic colleagues at other museums and enterprising dealers began to propose exciting new shows, French typically

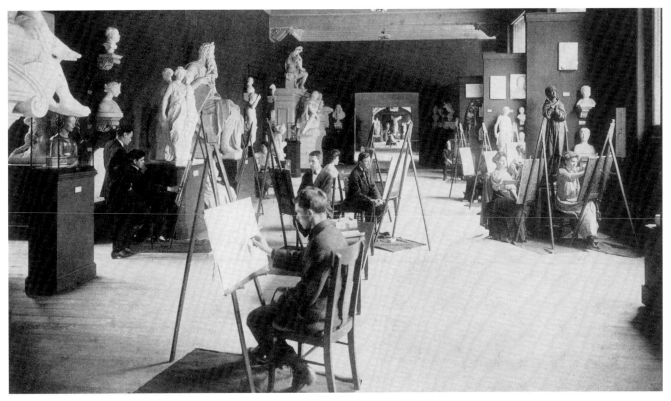

FIGURE 6. A coeducational class from the School of the Art Institute sketching in the sculpture galleries of the museum's Allerton Building. In the mid- to late nineteenth century, copying plaster casts was an essential part of artistic training. French considered the connection between the school and museum so strong that he was unwilling even to have a separate entrance for students, insisting that they must pass through the galleries to reach their classrooms. Collection of Celia Hilliard.

resisted their overtures: he had to proceed slowly, he needed more information, the costs were too great, the calendar was already booked. Frequently he cited legitimate difficulties with customs law, whereby only bond was required for paintings imported solely for exhibition, but duty was owed in advance on those intended for sale. (The possibility of sales was always a key incentive to participation for artists working abroad, who were typically wary of the packing, bureaucratic tasks, and hazards of transporting art over long distances.) Sometimes French simply admitted that he didn't like the modern works. "The jaded taste of the east may stand in need of them," he told one dealer, "but the fresh and fleecy west can get along without them."[15]

With the board's approval, the Art Institute did show contemporary art, but for several years every single exhibition originated elsewhere. A 1906 show of German art, from which the Chicagoan Fritz von Frantzius purchased

Franz von Stuck's *Salome* (FIG. 7), came through the efforts of Charles M. Kurtz, the exuberant director of the Albright Art Gallery in Buffalo. The work of "The Eight" (known as the Ashcan School) was shown in an exhibit initiated by the Pennsylvania Academy of the Fine Arts. In 1909 the collector Hugo Reisinger brought to Chicago a spectacular exhibit of contemporary German art that included works by Arnold Böcklin, Max Liebermann (FIG. 8), Adolph Menzel, and Hans Thoma. Reisinger suggested some pieces for the museum to acquire, including Hans von Bartels's striking large watercolor *The Pardon in Brittany*, which French dutifully—but unenthusiastically—showed Hutchinson. After the Art Institute declined to purchase anything, the watercolor was immediately acquired by Chicago collector James Deering. Another remarkable event was the exhibition of the Société Nouvelle, an eclectic confederation of painters and sculptors who had risen to prominence at the New Salon in Paris

FIGURE 7. Franz von Stuck (German, 1863–1928). *Salome*, 1906. Oil on canvas; 114.5 x 92 cm (51 ¹³⁄₁₆ x 36 ³⁄₁₆ in.). Staedtische Galerie im Lenbachhaus und Kunstbau München. Fritz von Frantzius, the Chicago collector who acquired this canvas, offered it to the Art Institute. It hung in the galleries briefly, until Hutchinson, who found the painting "pretty disagreeable," retired it to a storeroom. After the death of Von Frantzius in 1917, the museum tried to purchase it, but his family refused.

FIGURE 8. Max Liebermann (German, 1847–1935). *The Flax Barn at Laren*, 1887. Oil on canvas; 135 x 232 cm (53 ⅛ x 91 ⅜ in.). Nationalgalerie, Staatliche Museen, Berlin, A I 431. Photo courtesy of Bildarchiv Preussischer Kulturbesitz / Art Resource, NY.

some years before. Organized by the unquenchable Cornelia B. Sage, who became director of the Albright Art Gallery after Kurtz's death, the show featured almost one hundred modern French pictures, including four from the Musée du Luxembourg, which was usually averse to granting any loans at all. Auguste Rodin, who was president of the group, sent three of his own small bronzes as well as ten Symbolist paintings by his late friend Eugène Carrière, whose work had never before been exhibited in America. French accepted the show for the museum but observed to R. C. Holland, head of the Saint Louis Art Museum, "Miss Sage deals much in superlatives."[16]

By 1911 a new generation of affluent Chicago collectors with progressive tastes had begun to effectively influence the deliberations of the art committee and demanded Hutchinson's attention. The head of this group was Arthur T. Aldis, who with his wife, Mary, had established a kind of salon at their compound in Lake Forest, with a barn-turned-theater and cottages for visiting artists and poets. Aldis's cohorts included the sons of Hutchinson's good friends, including Robert Allerton, Frederic Clay Bartlett, Kenneth Sawyer Goodman, Abram Poole, and George F. Porter. Going straight over the head of French (who in any case found Aldis "wild and radical"), they suggested that Sara Hallowell's taste was outdated, her contacts stale, and the Art Institute's autumn show need not be dominated by the Salons of Paris.[17] Thus the trustees began to seriously consider discontinuing their use of Hallowell's services. Aldis proposed instead that they should supplement her findings with new work from Munich and Madrid. Ethel Coe, a teacher at the School of the Art Institute who was then studying with Joaquín and Sorolla, was asked to assemble and send over a small exhibition of Spanish art, which eventually opened in May 1913 to an enthusiastic response. The innovations made by this group did not end there. George F. Porter, on his part, wanted the museum to host a series of solo shows starting with work by painter and pastellist Henri Le Sidaner. Aldis and Poole

FIGURE 9. Students from the School of the Art Institute protesting the Armory Show outside the museum on April 16, 1913, the closing day of the exhibition. They staged a mock trial of Henri Matisse and burned copies of three of his paintings. Local professional artists also disapproved. Members of the Cliff Dwellers Club staged a satirical exhibition, with high marks given to Lorado Taft's revision of the display's most renowned painting (Marcel Duchamp's *Nude Descending a Staircase*) as *Nude Eating a Soup with a Fork*.

contacted Fritz Ehler, Ferdinand Hodler, Gustav Klimt, and Leo Samberger, relying on officials at the Neue Pinakothek in Munich for help. Together they discovered portraitist Romaine Brooks, although they cautioned French that the matter of exhibiting her canvases must be "left exclusively in our hands for the time being."[18] Kenneth Sawyer Goodman was even appointed curator of prints, although he served without salary. While he was lax about mundane but necessary practical tasks, it was largely through his urging that drawings and etchings by Aubrey Beardsley, Will Rothenstein, and a host of contemporary German graphic artists were seen at the museum. In time a large number of collectors and trustees acquired the power to choose exhibitions, curate shows, and supervise installations, muddling the budget and confusing the lines of institutional authority.

The controversy surrounding the famous International Exhibition of Modern Art (the Armory Show) was in some ways the most visible outcome of these long-brewing developments. The 1913 exhibition was the first appearance of Post-Impressionist and Cubist art in America, and unsurprisingly, its stop in Chicago had been instigated by Arthur T. Aldis, who first suggested the city as a venue to the show's organizers in 1911. French, perhaps at last eager to win over "our rich friends," as he described this new group of museum supporters, proposed to Hallowell that the Art Institute carefully select a small collection of such works to eliminate contentious subjects and show modern art without seeming to endorse it.[19] She declined the task, and French seemed delighted to inform her, "Mr. Hutchinson is a good deal interested in your comments on the 'Cubistes' and 'Futuristes,' and appeared to sympathize with them."[20] Nevertheless, plans continued to include Chicago on the circuit for the Armory Show, and on the eve of departure for his annual trip abroad, Hutchinson called a special meeting of the art committee to authorize the exhibition and the deinstallation of several major galleries to make space for it (FIG. 1). Although he visited his wife's relatives in California for the duration of the show's stay in Chicago, French did

FIGURE 10. Maurice de Vlaminck (French, 1876–1958). *Village*, c. 1912. Oil on canvas; 73.7 x 92.1 cm (29 x 36 ¼ in.). Arthur Jerome Eddy Memorial Collection, 1931.517. Eddy not only acquired works such as this from the Armory Show, but also explained and defended the art on display in a public lecture in Fullerton Hall, from which hundreds were turned away.

the flora. Chicago has often been mocked for its seemingly unsophisticated response to the exhibition, but it should be noted that the show drew the same reaction in New York (where it was denounced as "freakish"), and the Art Institute was the only museum to welcome it.[24] Moreover, the Chicago collector Arthur Jerome Eddy obtained at least twenty of its works, George F. Porter bought two, and Mary Aldis acquired multiple examples of graphic art. The Friends of American Art even ventured a purchase: an oil portrait by the feminist author and illustrator Mary A. Hallock Foote. Several midwestern museum directors journeyed to see the show and afterward pressed Eddy to loan the art he had purchased, which included works by Duchamp, Francis Picabia, Jacques Villon, and Maurice de Vlaminck (FIG. 10). On his return from California, French, relieved to have escaped the pandemonium, declared that at least "the public now knows the worst."[25] In truth, the show had the opposite effect, initiating a surprising reversal of roles. Impressed by the Art Institute's progressivism, museums all over the country considered it a trendsetter and clamored to host exhibitions it was planning.

* * *

With the outbreak of war in Europe, many ambitious plans were unfortunately disrupted. French's unexpected death from cancer in June 1914 was a wrenching loss despite the trials and discordant strains of recent years. Once the United States entered the war, the museum leadership necessarily focused on coping with labor and material shortages, and by 1918 a coal shortage forced the Art Institute to adopt early closing hours. At the same time, the museum made many positive contributions to the war effort (FIG. 11). Uniformed service members always received free admission, and Saturday evening dances were held for the soldiers and sailors billeted in Grant Park. There were also free lectures, a series of war-related exhibits, and some impressive symposia,

see it in New York, where he perceived the full extent of its strange and radical impact. Writing to Hutchinson, who was then in Paris, he pronounced it "a large element of hoax and humbug, and another large element of laziness and incompetence. The extreme works I take to be intentional jokes."[21]

When it opened in Chicago, the Armory Show, which embraced works by Paul Cézanne, Marcel Duchamp, Paul Gaugin, Vincent van Gogh, Henri Matisse, Pablo Picasso, and Odilon Redon, among many others, immediately drew raucous crowds and vitriolic commentary (FIG. 9). On free days attendance varied between 13,000 and 18,000 visitors, and hundreds were turned away from lectures arguing for and against the art on display. A circus spirit pervaded the galleries, with hard-boiled reporters griping, "Hanging is too good for some of these pictures."[22] One member of the museum staff reported to French, "In room 50 yesterday I heard a man laugh at the top of his voice. He inflamed the entire company, and everybody roared."[23] In a comic fluke, the annual flower show was simultaneously in session, and its managers expressed concerns that the pictures would kill

FIGURE 11. Recruitment rally outside the Art Institute during World War I. The museum supported the war effort in various ways. For example, its South Terrace was used as a reviewing stand for a parade of drafted men on August 4, 1917, and during the war soldiers and sailors in uniform, along with "any ladies who may accompany them," received free admission.

including an all-day forum on government use of art in war featuring artists, military personnel, and music by the Great Lakes Naval Band. As might be expected, Hutchinson served as master of ceremonies for many of these events.

However, the war seems to have had a profoundly dispiriting effect on him. He had at first hoped and argued for peace. In 1915 some of his friends were shocked to see him, a lifelong Republican and America booster, standing on the platform beside Jane Addams as she fought to advance the harshly derided peace movement, and he was one of the first to join the Illinois State Committee of the League to Enforce Peace.[26] Once the United States was embroiled in the hostilities, Hutchinson predictably immersed himself

in a host of service organizations. He was treasurer of several funds supporting the Red Cross, American Ambulance Service, and Permanent Blind Relief, and his exhaustive efforts on behalf of Belgian orphans and refugees earned him a knighthood at the end of the war. As befit his fervent commitment to the preservation of historic monuments, he was a leader of the campaign to restore the great cathedral at Rheims, an endeavor begun even while the city was still under daily German shellfire. But despite this active schedule of commitments, Hutchinson was showing signs of slow but certain decline. Throughout their wartime correspondence, friends cautioned him to take care of his health.

"HIS MOST PERMANENT MONUMENT"

AFTER THE WAR, energies at the museum were most visibly employed in planning a large addition to accommodate its collections, which were expanding rapidly both in their nature and size.[1] Construction of a bridge over the Illinois Central Railroad tracks had begun as early as 1912, although the work repeatedly came to a halt until the Art Institute firmly established its legal right to enlarge its presence in the park. In January 1920, Hutchinson was finally authorized to obtain working drawings and cost estimates for a "terrace addition" to be built immediately east of the new bridge, an extremely expensive proposition. The following year, George A. McKinlock, founder and president of the Central Electric Company, was searching for a suitable memorial for his son, who had been killed in action at the battle of Berzy-le-Sac. He offered to fund the sunken garden and its surrounding terraces, later increasing his donation to embellish the court with statuary (FIG. 2). In conjunction with an intensive fundraising drive, McKinlock's gift enabled this major project to move ahead. Years before, the trustees had dedicated the Hutchinson Gallery of Old Masters in honor of Charles's twenty-fifth anniversary as president (FIG. 3). In further appreciation, they now proposed to designate the new complex the Hutchinson Wing, a tribute perhaps all the more urgent as he seemed weaker by the day. When longtime trustee William O. Goodman expressed a desire to build a theater east of the addition, in memory of his son Kenneth Sawyer Goodman, who died in the 1918 influenza epidemic, it was clear that the Art Institute was well positioned for enormous growth in the years ahead.

Filling the position of director after French's death proved more problematic. Hutchinson tried to recruit Philip J. Gentner, the brilliant head of the Worcester Art Museum, for which he had acquired a group of notable American and European works. Gentner, who was then living part of the year in Florence, declined.[2] As a result, the directorship was temporarily occupied by Newton Carpenter, an acknowledged "plain businessman" with a modest knowledge of art but a genius for promoting it.[3] In 1916 George W. Eggers (FIG. 4) was appointed acting director for one year, which suggests that the trustees had reservations about his long-term prospects from the beginning. Eggers ultimately occupied the position for four years, and did effectively reorganize the school, but this included cutting expenses, increasing tuition, and making many faculty changes, policies that prompted the retirement of its longest-serving teachers and the resignation of its dean. Accordingly, in 1920 Robert B. Harshe was brought from the Carnegie Institute to serve as head of the school and assistant director of the museum (FIG. 5). The genial Eggers, an aspiring artist primarily interested in study and travel, was quickly eclipsed by the masterful and energetic Harshe, who was promoted to associate director of the museum less than a year later. In July Eggers departed to head the Denver Art Museum and Harshe was offered the job of director.

He did not immediately accept the post. After a period of rumination, he was invited to lay out his concerns on paper. Stressing that what he had to say was "neither palatable or politic," he stated that he found the present state of administrative affairs unacceptable, although he understood it was the product of years of struggle, fallow periods, growth spurts, conflicts between different personalities, overlapping

FIGURE 1. Hutchinson at Wychwood, c. 1920.

FIGURE 2. The George Alexander McKinlock, Jr., Memorial Court, after remodeling and the installation of *Fountain of the Tritons*, 1926, by Carl Milles, c. 1931. The sunken garden, together with the galleries on the left, constituted the Hutchinson Wing, which was named by the trustees—along with the Hutchinson Gallery of Old Masters—to honor the president's years of service.

duties, and close personal ties—all of which made change difficult. The problem lay not only with interfering trustees and donors who confused and usurped administrative and curatorial functions. Staff members who bypassed or ignored management, withheld information, and retained keys, tools, and access to significant relationships were also a factor. Without clear authority to establish a professional atmosphere and take charge of the collections, Harshe doubted whether he could fulfill the requirements of a demanding job that, he wrote, "should be the second most important position in the American art world." His five-page single-spaced letter passed unwritten but clearly implied judgment on Hutchinson's longstanding prerogatives and all-encompassing authority.[4]

Harshe was a forthright and courageous man, but it is almost certain that he did not submit his blunt statement without already sensing he could count on the president's support. Indeed, whatever his regrets about ceding so much of his power, Hutchinson was prepared to relinquish the nearly complete control that he had enjoyed for almost forty

FIGURE 3. The Hutchinson Gallery of Old Masters, located in the south wing of the second floor, was dedicated in October 1907 to celebrate the twenty-fifth anniversary of Hutchinson's presidency.

FIGURE 4. George W. Eggers was appointed director of the Art Institute in 1916. He exceeded the trustees' initial expectations but departed in 1921 to lead the Denver Art Museum.

years because he saw that it was a necessary condition for the Art Institute's continued strength and growth. Harshe was appointed director on his own terms and went on to invigorate the acquisition and exhibition programs, refurbish the galleries, and invest in talented curators who began the long process of reshaping the culture and direction of the museum. Hutchinson's willingness to step aside and permit this development for the sake of the Art Institute should rank among his biggest triumphs.

* * *

Although joyous in many ways, Hutchinson's life was not without its private pain and disappointments. Some were long-standing. His wife Frances was an enthusiastic partner in many intellectual and artistic activities. Longtime chair of the Antiquarians' purchasing committee, she also established the Art Institute's costume collection in 1912, contributing many rare examples of mid-nineteenth-century clothing.[5] An avid reader, she wrote a smattering of poems and published three books on the couple's international travels and

country life at Wychwood.[6] However, some tensions existed between the pair. Less enamored of public life than her husband, Frances was restless for other worlds of adventure and excitement. She was captivated by literary celebrity and the glamorous side of cultural endeavors, as well as outsize physical thrills. Watching a lakefront air show in 1910, she longed for an airplane ride herself. "Mustn't it be a glorious sensation?" she wrote to a friend.[7] Following the couple's annual winter journey abroad, she preferred to linger in Europe on her own, sometimes not returning to Chicago before June or July. Hutchinson was thus consigned to many lonely days and weeks. Most poignant were his solitary birthdays, lightly marked by a cable greeting from Frances and a small gift (perhaps a pair of vest buttons or a bookholder) she had wrapped months before. At the Fortnightly of Chicago, a women's club at which members delivered papers on subjects of personal interest, Frances once presented an essay titled "Second Best," which seems to suggest her discontents and thwarted hopes. The Hutchinsons had no children, although Charles had several namesakes among those of his family and friends. One of these, a promising

FIGURE 5. Robert B. Harshe served as director of the Art Institute from 1921 to 1938. Despite the differences in their administrative styles, Hutchinson recognized his talent and embraced him as French's successor. Harshe was later declared the greatest museum director of his day.

departed. His business life was also in flux. He appeared to welcome the 1919 merger of the Corn Exchange with the Illinois Trust and Merchants Loan banks, although he might have felt a wistful twinge when the consolidation was completed and the name of the Corn Exchange slipped into oblivion.

Hutchinson had suffered severe gout attacks starting in his early forties. Now afflicted with painful arthritis, complicated by failing organs, he was scarcely able to walk without a cane. Despite his friends' alarm at his poor color and obvious frailty, he tried to carry on as usual at clubs, conferences, and church gatherings, but it was a struggle. On the envelope containing an invitation from the Rochester Memorial Art Gallery to address their donors in the dead of January, he penciled "Would make a wreck out of me."[9] Winters in a Pasadena bungalow offered some respite, but his favorite refuge was the quiet wilderness of Wychwood (FIGS. 1, 8). Making his way along the forest paths, where he knew the name of every fern, shrub, and wildflower, Hutchinson felt he was among the greatest collection of masterpieces he had ever beheld. He kept peanuts in his pocket for the squirrels and could sit transfixed for an hour watching a bird peck at an apple. He still delighted in playing host in the rustic house, with its screened porches, beamed ceilings, and full wine cellar. For many friends, the memory of Hutchinson that lingered longest was the picture of him arranging flowers on a Sunday morning, when they could catch a glimpse of the tender side "he was so shy about betraying."[10] Charles and Frances made a last European journey in the winter of 1924, spending nine weeks in the balmy air at Cannes. On June 23 he presided over his final trustees' meeting. After a difficult summer at Lake Geneva, he entered Presbyterian Hospital for observation, and following surgery he died there on October 7, 1924.

Hutchinson's will included an outright cash gift to the Art Institute and additional funds to be donated after the death of his wife. He also bequeathed twenty paintings, in which Frances chose to immediately surrender her

youth in his early twenties, took his own life, a tragedy that left its own indelible sorrow.[8]

Changes in later life also tested Hutchinson's trademark forbearance. In 1921 he was forced to abandon his beloved Prairie Avenue home. As fashionable Chicago moved to the Gold Coast in the first decades of the twentieth century, the neighborhood declined, and gradually the houses of his old friends were demolished, subdivided for commercial use, or converted to brothels and gambling dens. The Hutchinsons were among the last to leave, residing temporarily in a North Side flat while they waited for Howard Van Doren Shaw to finish construction of a deluxe apartment house at 2450 North Lakeview Avenue. By early 1924 they had moved in, occupying a twenty-two-room floor-through apartment on the seventh floor, just upstairs from Ernest Hamill and his wife and downstairs from Kate Buckingham, another old acquaintance and major Art Institute supporter. Even living among longtime friends, Hutchinson found it difficult to accept the fate of his Prairie Avenue homestead, which reopened as a boardinghouse shortly after he and Frances

FIGURE 6. Pablo Picasso (Spanish, 1881–1973). *Head of a Woman*, 1909. Gouache, with water-color, black and ocher chalks, stumping, and subtractive techniques on ivory laid paper; 62.5 x 48 cm (24 ⁵/₈ x 18 ⁷/₈ in.). Edward E. Ayer Endowment Fund in memory of Charles L. Hutchinson, 1945.136.

FIGURE 7. Ryerson, c. 1920. Following Hutchinson's death, the Art Institute trustees elected Ryerson honorary president for life. Chicago History Museum, iCHi-61816.

life interest.[11] Even while Charles was still alive, his friend Edward E. Ayer had established a fund in his honor that was subsequently used to purchase rare works by such masters as Alberto Giacometti, Henri Matisse, Piet Mondrian, and Pablo Picasso (FIG. 6).[12]

Hutchinson's death marked the end of an era at the museum and confirmed that a new one had begun. At the annual meeting following his passing, Ryerson was named, at his own request, an honorary trustee. The board then elected him honorary president for life, after which he attended fewer and fewer meetings (FIG. 7). Potter Palmer, Jr., was elected president and went on to serve for nineteen years. Generous, dedicated, and an avid collector himself, Palmer continued his predecessor's tradition of stopping in at the museum almost

every weekday, although it is telling that it was Harshe who inherited Hutchinson's impressive double partners desk.

But these events signaled more than just a transformation in the division of power at the Art Institute. Rather, Hutchinson's death and Harshe's ascendancy typified a sea change taking place in museums across the United States, as the amateur enthusiasts and gentleman collectors who founded these organizations were replaced by a new generation of trained specialists. The informal infrastructure and staffing of museums in their first fifty or so years was in part simply a product of the times; the concept of the professional in today's sense had only recently emerged, even in fields such as medicine, and was unheard of in comparatively new areas such as the public display of art. But the casual organization of museums was also a product of their origins as the creations of men who belonged to a class in which social and financial affairs were intertwined, who considered art a civilizing, even elevating force, and who enjoyed the leisure to devote their lives to its support and promotion. Under such circumstances, the worlds of business and pleasure, public and private merged. Hutchinson and Ryerson—who were friends as well as colleagues—traveled around the world for their own enjoyment, but they also used their trips to familiarize themselves with methods of display and to obtain works for the Art Institute, sometimes paying for the objects themselves or enlisting their friends to help.[13] Hutchinson's daily schedule reflected the close connection of his business, personal, philanthropic, and professional lives.[14] He spent the vast majority of his time at the museum, usually fulfilling responsibilities such as meeting with French or touring the facilities, but also frequently engaging in charitable or social events. Moreover, whether at the Corn Exchange Bank, concerts, dinners, or plays, Hutchinson encountered the same men with whom he worked at the Art Institute.

Beginning in the early twentieth century, however, the relaxed culture fostered by these friendly relationships began to be replaced by more bureaucratic arrangements. Certainly the simple passage of time was a factor; as the founding generation retired or passed away, a new group of men stepped in to take their place. Though in most cases members of the same elite as their predecessors, these individuals had different ideas about what museums could and should do. Where Hutchinson's generation talked of the elevating power of art in a way that sometimes suggested the public must come to it, the new generation spoke of service, conceiving their mission as bringing art to the people.[15] This change in outlook stemmed in part from these men's self-identification not as patrons but as professionals who prized efficiency and specialized training. Broad social changes such as the increase in immigration and the rise of the Progressive movement also contributed to their outlook.

These men and their new way of conducting business were able to find a home in American museums because of changes in these organizations themselves. Just as the surrounding cities had grown and matured over the past decades, so too had the institutions. Much larger, both physically due to ambitious building campaigns and in the size and scope of their collections thanks to the generosity of their supporters, they had become more complex and expensive to run, and required the attention of professionals to meet their administrative and financial needs. In a sense, the founders displaced themselves through the very success of their endeavor.

Hutchinson belonged firmly in the earlier era of museums but, in his ideals, he also anticipated the next. At a memorial service held in Fullerton Hall on November 26, 1924, several speakers paid tribute to his character, clarity of vision, energy, and devotion to the dream of a magnificent art museum to serve the people of Chicago. Indeed, by the end of his life, the phrases once used to describe his father applied equally to him. A "deep sagacious operator" in the service of his causes, "the main man" and "the ruling spirit" at the museum, his signature was indeed "gilt edge"—or at least gleaming enough to win the support of his peers for whatever endeavor he backed. Hutchinson had matched—even exceeded—his father's success in his own, quite different field. As Harshe declared, "He was the Art Institute and it will stand as his most permanent monument," or as French once said, he was "the prime mover in everything" at the museum.[16] Indeed, even more than the physical structures Hutchinson helped build and the art he worked to acquire, his most enduring legacy is the organization itself, a vessel sturdy enough to accommodate the achievements, ambitions, and hopes of generations far into the future. As Hutchinson himself once said, in words that suggest he shared the next generation's vision of museums more than is at first apparent, "Art is not destined for a small and privileged class. Art is democratic, it is of the people, and for the people and from the people have come some of its greatest creators. . . . The Art Museum of today, if it properly fulfills its function, is no longer a mere storehouse. It must offer to the public changing exhibitions of contemporaneous Art. It should be the center of the artistic activities of the community in which it exists. The most successful Art Museum of today is at once a storehouse, a college, and a general exchange for the Art of the whole community."[17]

FIGURE 8. Artist and poet Bertha Jaques, echoing the sentiments of many of Hutchinson's friends, wrote after his death, "I never think of him except with flowers in his hand. That picture will remain with me always."

NOTES

"THE ORIGINAL ART IMPULSE," pp. 8–17.

The title of this section comes from a remark by Charles L. Hutchinson's friend Calvin Cobb: "You did have her snakeship in marble, which you should treasure as the original art impulse." Birthday calendar 1915, vol. 1, page for May 24, Hutchinson Personal Papers, Art Institute of Chicago Archives (hereafter cited as AIC Archives).

1. "Charles Lawrence Hutchinson," *Bulletin of the Art Institute of Chicago* 28, 9 (Dec. 1924), p. 110.

2. "Simplicity Marks Hutchinson Funeral," *Chicago Daily News*, Oct. 9, 1924, p. 6.

3. For an in-depth examination of the ideas presented in this paragraph as they relate specifically to Chicago, see Helen Lefkowitz Horowitz, *Culture and the City: Cultural Philanthropy in Chicago from the 1880s to 1917* (University Press of Kentucky, 1976).

4. Chicago Exhibition of the Fine Arts, *First Exhibition of Statuary, Paintings, etc.*, exh. cat. (Chicago Press and Tribune Print, 1859). Frederic Edwin Church's *View of Cotopaxi*, now in the collection of the Art Institute (1919.753), was first exhibited in this show.

5. French, "Mr. W. T. Baker and the Art Institute of Chicago," Aug. 3, 1906. French Papers, AIC Archives.

6. Joel S. Dryer, "The Story You Don't Know About a Place We All Love," paper delivered to the Chicago Literary Club, May 14, 2001.

7. French (note 5).

8. "Ladder to Success," *Chicago Inter Ocean*, Nov. 15, 1891, p. 9.

9. Edward A. Duddy, "Benjamin Peters Hutchinson," in Dumas Malone, ed., *Dictionary of American Biography*, vol. 9 (Charles Scribner's Sons, 1932), p. 437.

10. Handwritten credit reports, Illinois, vol. 34, p. 222, R. G. Dun and Company Collection, Baker Library Historical Collections, Harvard Business School. Other reports contained in this collection noted that B. P. Hutchinson was a "deep, sagacious operator" and that "his paper is gilt-edge." Elsewhere in these reports (Illinois, vol. 39, p. 319) he was identified as the "main man" and "the ruling spirit" among his several partners in the packing company.

11. Albert R. Sabin, "Tribute to the Memory of George Howland, Superintendent of Schools of City of Chicago 1880–1891," in *Thirty-Ninth Annual Report of the Board of Education of the City of Chicago*.

12. Birthday Calendar 1915, vol. 1, page for May 24, Hutchinson Personal Papers.

13. "Only Moneygrubbers?" *Chicago History* 6, 12 (Summer 1963), p. 377. Ryder was a scholar as well as a preacher. The library in his house on Michigan Avenue contained pictures, manuscripts, and two thousand books, including many rare volumes.

14. Thomas Wakefield Goodspeed, "Charles Lawrence Hutchinson," in *The University of Chicago Biographical Sketches*, vol. 2 (University of Chicago Press, 1925), p. 28.

15. Edward A. Duddy, "Charles Lawrence Hutchinson," in Malone (note 9), p. 438. No records survive to confirm who paid for these shares. Charles was by this time an able and well-compensated manager, but it is likely that a large portion of the shares he acquired were an outright gift from his father. Benjamin was the bank's major stockholder and had already bought a business for his son-in-law, giving him first half, and later full, ownership.

16. "Some Anecdotes of 'Old Hutch,'" unidentified newspaper clipping, 1899, scrapbook of clippings, box 3, Charles L. Hutchinson Manuscript Collection, Newberry Library, Chicago (hereafter cited as Hutchinson Collection).

17. Goodspeed (note 14), pp. 28–29.

18. "Highway and Byway," *Chicago Tribune*, Nov. 17, 1889, p. 27.

19. William Ferris, "Old Hutch—The Wheat King," *Journal of the Illinois State Historical Society* 41, 3 (Sept. 1948), p. 234.

20. Grace Murray Meeker, "Early Prairie Avenue," Members and Guests Papers (1873–1943), box 2, Fortnightly of Chicago Papers, Newberry Library, Chicago.

"A BRICKS AND MORTAR MAN," pp. 18–35.

Throughout his career, Hutchinson took a leading role in some of Chicago's most prominent building projects, including the campaigns to construct the Auditorium Theater, the Chicago Orphan Asylum, Orchestra Hall, and St. Paul's Universalist Church. His enthusiasm for such endeavors was widely noted by his colleagues. For example, French remarked, "We must continue to build in order to accommodate our activities and [Hutchinson's] mind is very much upon that." French to Garrett C. Pier, Apr. 22, 1908, French Papers.

1. Recently shown at the Inter-State Exposition, *Beheading of Saint John the Baptist* had been purchased and presented to the new museum by a group of men (publicly unidentified but including Hutchinson). In March 1950 the painting was placed at Mundelein College (now part of Loyola University, Chicago).

Frances Hutchinson and Carrie Ryerson in Yokohama, 1896. They are dressed in traditional Japanese kimonos and wear lacquered hair ornaments.

2. "The Display of Paintings," *Chicago Tribune*, Jan. 14, 1883, p. 9. Shown in another gallery was a handsome collection of Chinese porcelain, an anonymous loan from a citizen who had traveled many years in Asia.

3. "Sheridan's Tapestries," *Chicago Tribune*, Jan. 23, 1883, p. 8.

4. "A Choice Exhibit," *Chicago Tribune*, Feb. 15, 1885, p. 12.

5. *The Century* later reclaimed these illustrations.

6. Bart Ryckbosch, "Imagining the Art Institute: William M. R. French's Travel Notebook," *Art Institute of Chicago Museum Studies* 34, 2 (2008), pp. 78–79.

7. French to E. F. Mack, Mar. 17, 1914, French Papers.

8. A notable instance of the latter occurred in late 1882, when James Jackson Jarves, the scholar and first important collector of early Italian primitives, made a trip west, with a stop in Chicago. Around that time he wrote a letter to Luigi Palma di Cesnola, director of the Metropolitan Museum of Art in New York, about the possibility of selling what remained of his private collection to an unnamed "western museum now in the course of organization." Francis Steegmuller, *The Two Lives of James Jackson Jarves* (Yale University Press, 1951), p. 281. It cannot be known for certain whether Jarves was referring to the Art Institute, or if the museum ever seriously considered such a purchase. It would have been tempting, but in any case, unaffordable. The pictures, which included works bought at the famed 1880 sale at Prince Anatole Demidoff's palace in Florence, were not disposed of until 1884 when Liberty E. Holden, publisher of the Cleveland *Plain Dealer*, bought them out of an exhibition in Boston. When the Cleveland Museum of Art opened in 1916, the paintings were prominently featured in a room of their own built to resemble an Italian palazzo. A much-touted gift at the time, some of the paintings (as with so many celebrated canvases) were later reattributed, including a Madonna and Child, then ascribed to Leonardo da Vinci and now thought to be the work of an imitator. Evan H. Turner, ed., *Object Lessons: Cleveland Creates an Art Museum* (Cleveland Museum of Art, 1991), pp. 16–17.

9. Minutes, Sept. 7, 1885, Board of Trustees Records, AIC Archives.

10. John W. Root to Hutchinson, July 16, 1885, Hutchinson Collection.

11. This women's group, which was founded as an association to display and market a wide range of ceramics, textiles, and other well-crafted objects, later became the Antiquarians, an independent society that played a major role in building the Art Institute's decorative arts collections. For a history of the organization, see Celia Hilliard, "'Higher Things': Remembering the Early Antiquarians," *Art Institute of Chicago Museum Studies* 28, 2 (2002), pp. 6–21.

12. "The New Munkacsy," *New York Times*, Jan. 14, 1888, p. 5.

13. Perhaps the most important was George Hitchcock's painting *Flower Girl in Holland*, from Potter Palmer. An attractive combination of the contemporary French and Dutch styles, it was given a prominent place in the gallery, set up on its own easel, honoring both the painting and its donor. It remains in the Art Institute's collection to this day (1888.169).

14. For more on the history of the Art Institute's library, see Jack Perry Brown, "The Book in the City Beautiful: Scholarly Collections at the Art Institute of Chicago," *Art Institute of Chicago Museum Studies* 34, 2 (2008), pp. 6–17.

15. Another frequent speaker was Frederick Keppel of New York, a print dealer who sold many fine works on paper to Chicagoans and prepared a definitive summary of the Art Institute's etchings that was declared to be "almost a catalogue raisonne." "Art Notes," *Graphic* 5, 24 (Dec. 12, 1891), p. 388.

16. Adam Emory Albright, a painter and father of the artists Ivan and Malvin Albright, remembered it as the Art Institute's "first successful exhibit" in his book *For Art's Sake* (privately printed, 1953).

17. One-time admission fees had been doubled under an agreement that granted half the proceeds to the show's original sponsor, the American Art Association.

18. Though East Coast critics at first dismissed Chicago collectors as ignorant and gullible, they gradually developed a high regard for the holdings of James W. Ellsworth, Henry and Marshall Field, Levi Leiter, and Charles T. Yerkes. By 1890 the editors of the New York publication *The Collector* acknowledged that Potter Palmer's recent acquisitions had assumed a "truly regal character." *Collector* 2, 2 (Nov. 15, 1890), p. 23.

19. Yerkes also purchased work by Jan van Beers, Jean Charles Cazin, Pieter de Hooch, and Jean-Louis-Ernest Meissonier.

20. "Death of Henry Field," *Chicago Tribune*, Dec. 23, 1890, p. 1.

21. Other notable collectors included James H. Dole, an early trustee and partner of George Armour; Albert A. Munger, heir to a grain elevator fortune; and Henry J. Willing, a onetime partner of Marshall Field.

22. Reluctant to conclude the sale despite having already agreed to it, the princess escaped to the country. Ellsworth was forced to press money into the hands of her son and remove the painting himself from a shadowy corner of her drawing room. All Chicago society was fascinated by this story, which Ellsworth loved to relate at length. Ellsworth to Hutchinson, Aug. 18, 1889, Hutchinson Papers. See also "A Private Art Gallery," *Chicago Tribune*, Feb. 15, 1890, p. 12.

23. "Madame X," "News of the Society World," *Chicago Tribune*, May 19, 1912, p. B1.

24. Ellsworth also promised to personally cover the cost of sending European museum employees to unpack, install, and guard the art for the duration of the fair. In the late 1890s, declaring that Chicago's smoke was ruining his pictures, he left the city and moved among houses in New Jersey, New York City, and his home state, Ohio, as well as a thirteenth-century castle on the Lake of Lucerne and his grandest residence, the Villa Palmieri, in the hills overlooking Florence. Here, in what was once the residence of a family in Cosimo de Medici's circle, Ellsworth held court among visiting friends and art lovers, including the Hutchinsons and Ryersons. He died at the villa in June 1925.

25. Frances Hutchinson also remembered that the first picture her husband ever bought "was an excellent study of a cat, a photograph." Paul Wright, "Charles L. Hutchinson: His Long Labors for His Home City," *Chicago Daily News*, Dec. 3, 1923, p. 8.

26. "Ladder to Success," *Chicago Inter Ocean*, Nov. 15, 1891, p. 9.

27. J. W. Beck to Hutchinson, July 26, 1886, Hutchinson Collection.

28. It appears that Hutchinson also made Watts's acquaintance at some point, either in person or through correspondence. In 1890, presumably as a gift and gesture of friendship, he commissioned for Watts, who was also an accomplished sculptor, a set of Leonard Volk's life casts of Abraham Lincoln's face and hands. Leonard Volk to Hutchinson, Oct. 17, 1890; Nov. 5, 1890; Jan. 7, 1891; Jan. 16, 1891, Hutchinson Collection.

29. "Rossetti's 'Beata Beatrix,'" *Chicago Tribune*, Nov. 27, 1887, p. 19.

30. "Art Matters in Chicago," *Chicago Tribune*, Dec. 1, 1889, p. 27.

31. "The Art Institute Gallery," *Chicago Tribune*, Dec. 29, 1889, p. 12.

32. "Art Notes," *Graphic* 12, 10 (Mar. 8, 1890), p. 151, includes a quote from a letter that William Holman Hunt wrote to French. This argument did not sway Chicagoans, however, and the painting returned to the artist. He continued to rework it, and *The Triumph of the Innocents* eventually found a home in the collection of the Walker Art Gallery, Liverpool. A later replica is in the British national collection and is housed in the Tate Britain, London. An earlier study is held by the Fogg Art Museum, Harvard University Art Museums, Cambridge.

33. Draft of a tribute to Hutchinson, undated typescript, University of Chicago, Office of the President, Harper, Judson, and Burton administrations, records (hereafter cited as Harper, Judson, and Burton Records), box 82, folder 13, Special Collections Research Center, University of Chicago Library.

34. Thomas J. Schlereth, "Big Money and High Culture: The Commercial Club and Charles L. Hutchinson," *Great Lakes Review* 3 (Summer 1976), pp. 15–27.

35. The Chicago Historical Society also sought space in this grand building, though over time both it and the city's public library—which Hutchinson had briefly brought on board as a partner—dropped their efforts to be included.

36. James Fentress to Stuyvesant Fish, Apr. 15, 1891, Presidents' Papers (Stuyvesant Fish), vol. 78, Illinois Central Railroad Company Archives (1851–1906), Newberry Library, Chicago.

37. "The Art Palace," *Chicago Herald*, undated newspaper clipping, scrapbook of clippings, box 3, Hutchinson Collection.

"PICTURE EXCITEMENT," pp. 36–45.

The title of this section comes from a contemporary newspaper article. See note 11 below.

1. French, "Art Students Abroad," *Chicago Tribune*, Apr. 21, 1889, p. 33.

2. Hutchinson to William Rainey Harper, Feb. 18, 1892, Harper, Judson, and Burton Records, box 82, folder 12.

3. French (note 1).

4. "Ladder to Success," *Chicago Inter Ocean*, Nov. 15, 1891, p. 9.

5. "Ecco Roma" was traditionally uttered by pilgrims as they caught their first glimpse of the dome of St. Peter's Basilica on approaching Rome. A friend of Hutchinson's wrote him, "I well remember when first those words of wondrous meaning to me were sounded—Ecco Roma! I know they thrilled you and your good wife with new experiences." E. W. Blatchford to Hutchinson, Dec. 14, 1889, Hutchinson Collection.

6. Hutchinson began a diary on his wedding day, May 26, 1881, but apparently abandoned the effort by the end of that year. He resumed writing on March 27, 1890, the eve of his and Frances's departure for Europe, and described events of the journey until the start of negotiations for the Demidoff collection in Paris. In January 1900, he restarted the journal again, this time writing regularly for over a decade. Although most of the individual entries from this period are not more than a line or two, they vividly portray the crowded calendar of a public man of affairs. Box 1, Hutchinson Collection.

7. Thomas Wakefield Goodspeed, "Charles Lawrence Hutchinson," in *The University of Chicago Biographical Sketches*, vol. 2 (University of Chicago Press, 1925), p. 45.

8. For an account of the Demidoff family collections and their dispersion, see Francis Haskell, "Anatole Demidoff and the Wallace Collection," in *Anatole Demidoff, Prince of San Donato (1812–70)*, Collectors of the Wallace Collection 1 (Trustees of the Wallace Collection, 1994), pp. 8–32.

9. "Famous Pictures for Chicago," *Chicago Tribune*, July 3, 1890, p. 3.

10. Other artists represented were Gerard ter Borch, Frans van Mieris, Adriaen van Ostade, Jacob van Ruysdael, David Teniers the Younger, William van de Velde, and Reinier Zeeman.

11. L. K., "Art Topics in France," *New York Times*, July 6, 1890, p. 12.

12. These pictures were purchased at the G. Rothan and M. Prosper Crabbe sales, two of a series of auctions held in Paris that spring which lifted prices for Old Master paintings to stupendous new levels.

13. Marcia Winn, "Art Institute Monument to City's Culture," *Chicago Tribune*, Feb. 3, 1946, p. 1.

14. Hutchinson recommended that a bequest from Frederick W. Crosby, a director of the Corn Exchange National Bank, be applied toward the cost of the last unfunded painting, Peter Paul Rubens's *Portrait of the Marquis de Spinola*. Crosby's widow, Jennie Norton Crosby, made an additional cash donation to establish the gift in his name. When she gave the final installment in 1935, the painting, whose attribution was then in doubt, was withdrawn and given to her.

"A COMMITTEE OF TWO," pp. 46–67.

The title of this section comes from a remark made by a member of the Art Institute's board of trustees. Minutes, Mar. 6, 1891, Board of Trustees Records, AIC Archives.

1. Halsey C. Ives to Hutchinson, n.d., Hutchinson Papers.

2. For French's comments about the proper lighting of paintings and sculpture, see French to the Director of the Washington State Art Association, May 31, 1912; French to Charles A. Coolidge, May 4, 1910; and French to Daniel Chester French, Mar. 8, 1912, all French Papers.

3. Hutchinson had apparently had another artist in mind, but Kemeys received the commission. See Bryan Lathrop to Charles L. Hutchinson, Sept. 24, 1892, Hutchinson Papers.

4. Thomas Wakefield Goodspeed, "Charles Lawrence Hutchinson," in *The University of Chicago Biographical Sketches*, vol. 2 (University of Chicago Press, 1925), p. 42.

5. "Gallery of Local Celebrities. No. XXX. Charles L. Hutchinson," *Chicago Tribune*, p. 47.

6. "No More Speculation," *Chicago Tribune*, Jan. 23, 1891, p. 1. See also "Did Not Intend to Confine Him," *Chicago Tribune*, May 2, 1891, p. 2.

7. "Some Anecdotes of 'Old Hutch,'" unidentified newspaper clipping, 1889, scrapbook of clippings, box 3, Hutchinson Collection.

8. For an account of Hutchinson property transfers on Prairie Avenue, see "Real Estate," *Chicago Tribune*, July 4, 1880, p. 11. See also Margaretta E. Otis, interview by Vivien Marie Palmer, July 1927, published as "Document #3a" in Chicago History Museum, *History of the Near South Side Community, Chicago*. Otis stated, "'Old Hutch,' Charles Hutchinson's father, was unable to buy land [on upper Prairie Avenue], so went south and started Lower Prairie Avenue." For a fine illustrated account of the street in its heyday, see William H. Tyre, *Chicago's Historic Prairie Avenue* (Arcadia Publishing, 2008).

9. Frances Macbeth Glessner and John J. Glessner Journals (1879–1921) (hereafter cited as Glessner Journals), entry for Feb. 6, 1887, Chicago History Museum.

10. Nancy Atwood Sprague to Frances Glessner, Sept. 11, 1887, Glessner Journals.

11. Kenyon Cox, "The Collection of Charles L. Hutchinson," August Jaccaci Papers (1889–1935), Archives of American Art, Washington, D. C.

12. Paul Wright, "Charles L. Hutchinson: His Long Labors For His Home City," *Chicago Daily News*, Dec. 3, 1923, p. 8.

13. Lake Geneva Gardener's and Foremen's Association, *Report of the Second Annual Chrysanthemum Show*, Lake Geneva, Wis., Nov. 9–10, 1906, Hutchinson Collection.

14. "Gallery of Local Celebrities" (note 5).

15. Entry for Jan. 26, 1896, Glessner Journals.

16. Zulima Taft Garland to Frances K. Hutchinson, n.d., memorial scrapbook, box 1, Hutchinson Papers.

17. St. Paul's Universalist Church, erected in 1887 at 3005 South Prairie Avenue, included a handsome chapel funded by Hutchinson and his friend Harlow N. Higinbotham. In 1919 the church relocated, with Hutchinson's financial and strategic assistance, to Sixtieth Street and Dorchester Avenue on land owned by the University of Chicago. It now houses the Sonia Shankman Orthogenic School.

18. John D. Rockefeller to Mr. and Mrs. Charles L. Hutchinson, Oct. 4, 1901, Hutchinson Collection.

19. Minutes, Mar. 6, 1891, Board of Trustees Records, AIC Archives.

20. John J. Glessner, *Should Auld Acquaintance Be Forgot?* (R. R. Donnelley and Sons at the Lakeside Press, 1924), p. 28.

21. The elder Martin Ryerson was elected a trustee of the Chicago Academy of Fine Arts in May 1880 and served one three-year term. Thereafter he supported the institution as a governing member. Paintings from his collection were exhibited at the Inter-State Exposition starting in 1873.

22. Goodspeed (note 4), p. 42.

23. Susan Hale to Hutchinson, May 24, 1889, Hutchinson Collection.

24. Isabella Stewart Gardner to Frances Glessner, Nov. 19, 1903, Glessner Journals.

25. For a discussion of Wychwood's architects (Charles Coolidge, John Olmsted, and Robert Spencer) and Hutchinson's subsequent influence on the development of adjoining estates, see John K. Notz, Jr., "Charles L. Hutchinson and His Design Professionals," paper delivered to the Chicago Literary Club, Nov. 19, 2001.

26. Frances Kinsley Hutchinson, *Motoring in the Balkans: Along the Highways of Dalmatia, Montenegro, the Herzegovina, and Bosnia* (A. C. McClurg, 1909).

27. Charles L. Hutchinson Diaries (hereafter cited as Hutchinson Diaries), Hutchinson Collection.

28. Edward G. Holden, "Chicago Anecdotes of Whistler," *Chicago Tribune*, July 19, 1903, p. 2.

29. Stanley R. Osborn, "Chicagoans at Play No. 6: Martin Ryerson, Connoisseur," *Chicago Record-Herald*, Oct. 22, 1913, p. 5.

30. Robert Morss Lovett, *All Our Years* (Viking Press, 1948), pp. 82–83. Higher criticism is a type of literary analysis used in biblical and Classical studies. It focuses on the origins of a work, as opposed to lower (or textual) criticism, whose goal is to identify what a text originally said before it was corrupted by transmission.

31. Hutchinson diaries, Hutchinson Collection. Hutchinson gives the date of his visit as May 26, 1900. His description of the experience (in two versions) is inserted at the end of his diary notes for the year 1900.

32. Hutchinson to Frances Glessner, Jan. 19, 1896, Glessner Journals.

33. Ryerson to William Rainey Harper, Feb. 23, 1896, Harper, Judson, and Burton Records, box 82, folder 23.

34. Hutchinson to William Rainey Harper, Feb. 18 and Feb. 28, 1892, Harper, Judson, and Burton Records, box 82, folder 12.

35. For a discussion of antiquities purchases in the early years of the museum, see Karen Alexander, "A History of the Ancient Art Collection at The Art Institute of Chicago," *Art Institute of Chicago Museum Studies* 20, 1 (1994), pp. 6–13.

36. Hutchinson diaries, entry for Jan. 1910, Hutchinson Collection.

37. French to Harrison S. Morris, Jan. 8, 1906, French Papers.

38. "The Art Institute of Chicago," unsigned typescript, Oct. 13, 1939, AIC Archives.

39. Stickney's own collection had been organized to form the core of a new prints and engravings department.

40. "M'Kay's Will Leaves $300,000 To Charity," *Chicago Tribune*, Nov. 26, 1914, p. 20.

41. French to Sara Hallowell, Jan. 29, 1910, French Papers.

42. Louisine W. Havemeyer, *Sixteen to Sixty: Memoirs of a Collector* (1930; repr., Ursus Press, 1993), p. 153.

43. Ibid.

44. Ibid., p. 155.

45. Grace Gassette to Hutchinson, Feb. 16, 1904, Hutchinson Collection.

46. Mary Cassatt to Hutchinson, Jan. 9, 1905, Hutchinson Papers.

47. French to Mrs. Samuel M. Nickerson, June 11, 1906, French Papers.

48. French to Hutchinson, Mar. 2, 1909, French Papers.

"THE CONSTANT IMPROVER," pp. 68–77.

The title of this section comes from Frances Kinsley Hutchinson's book *Wychwood*: "'You need not imagine, my dear inexperienced friend, that you can ever really finish a country place,' replied the Constant Improver, for so was re-christened The Man Who Had Always Wanted a Farm. 'That is one of its greatest charms. There is always something new to make, to build, to do.'" Frances Kinsley Hutchinson, *Wychwood: The History of an Idea* (Lakeside Press, 1928), p. 8.

1. Ryerson to Hutchinson, Apr. 16, 1912, Hutchinson Collection.

2. For an analysis of Martin Ryerson as a collector, see two excellent discussions: Martha Wolff's introduction in Christopher Lloyd et al., *Italian Paintings Before 1600 in the Art Institute of Chicago: A Catalogue of the Collection* (Art Institute

of Chicago/Princeton University Press, 1993), pp. xi–xvi; and Neil Harris, "Midwestern Medievalism: Three Chicago Collectors," in Isabella Stewart Gardner Interdisciplinary Symposium, *Cultural Leadership in America: Art Matronage and Patronage, Isabella Stewart Gardner Museum*, Fenway Court 27 (Isabella Stewart Gardner Museum, 1997), pp. 104–24.

3. In 1900 Hutchinson bought Henry Ward Ranger's cityscape *Brooklyn Bridge* (1925.720), a showpiece of the American exhibit at the Exposition universelle in Paris. He remained interested in Ranger's work and acquired his *Noank Shipyards* in 1904. Hutchinson was also friendly with another Tonalist painter, Ben Foster, and the American Impressionist Frank Weston Benson, and may have purchased examples of their work. He continued to buy contemporary American pewter, pottery, and silver, and European and American commemorative medals. Most of his personal art collection, however, was acquired before the turn of the century.

4. Hutchinson to John J. Glessner, July 6, 1915, Glessner Journals. Hutchinson also received honorary master of arts and doctor of laws degrees from Tufts University, which was founded as a nonsectarian institution by the Universalist Church.

5. Lorado Taft, a teacher and lecturer at the Art Institute, acknowledged the importance of Hutchinson's support throughout his career. In 1912 he proposed another Ferguson Fund sculpture, *Fountain of Time*, to beautify the Midway Plaisance on Chicago's South Side. Hutchinson urged this project over the objections of the landscape architect John Olmsted, nephew and adopted son of Frederick Law Olmsted, whose original vision for the space included a Venetian canal lined by trees and green lawns.

6. French to Garrett C. Pier, Apr. 22, 1908, French Papers. The full quotation reads, "Certainly the collection which you describe is important enough to arrest anybody's attention. I submitted the matter to Mr. Hutchinson, who as you know is the prime mover in everything here."

7. French to Albert S. Ludlow, Aug. 19, 1911, French Papers.

8. Hutchinson, untitled address delivered to an unidentified audience, c. 1917, Hutchinson Manuscript Collection.

9. For a discussion of Bennett's singular career, see Bart H. Ryckbosch, "Bessie Bennett," in *Women Building Chicago, 1790–1990: A Biographical Dictionary*, ed. Rima Lunin Schultz and Adele Hast (Indiana University Press, 2001), pp. 77–80.

10. French to Mary Van Horne, July 23, 1912, French Papers.

11. French to Halsey C. Ives, May 28, 1909, French Papers.

12. French to Sara Hallowell, July 1, 1909, French Papers.

13. French to Sara Hallowell, Sept. 5, 1907, French Papers.

14. When Harriet Monroe first sought subscribers in 1911 for *Poetry*, her new magazine of modernist verse, Hutchinson assured her, "You may count on me as long as I live." Harriet Monroe, *A Poet's Life: Seventy Years in a Changing World* (MacMillan Company, 1938), p. 244. Hutchinson was among those who introduced the Irish poet William Butler Yeats at a large dinner Monroe hosted for Yeats at the Cliff Dwellers Club in March 1914.

15. French to Martin Birnbaum, July 23, 1912, French Papers.

16. French to R. A. Holland, Aug. 30, 1913, French Papers.

17. French to Sara Hallowell, Nov. 25, 1912, French Papers.

18. French to Sara Hallowell, Apr. 14, 1914, French Papers. French relayed to Hallowell Aldis's wish that he and Abram Poole have exclusive control over communications with Brooks.

19. French to Sara Hallowell, Feb. 3, 1912, French Papers.

20. French to Sara Hallowell, Apr. 6, 1912, French Papers.

21. French to Hutchinson, Mar. 20, 1913, French Papers.

22. Charles H. Burkholder to French, Apr. 8, 1913, French Papers. The Armory Show drew scorn from not only much of the press, the public, and local artists, but also some of the Art Institute's own students.

23. Charles H. Burkholder to French, Mar. 27, 1913, French Papers.

24. An article in the *Chicago Tribune* related, "On Tuesday the public will be admitted to see that style of art which severe critics in New York and elsewhere have termed 'freakish' and 'deformatory.'" "'Famous Cubists' Collection Here Talked of 'Freak' Paintings Reach Institute for Exhibition Next Week," *Chicago Tribune*, Mar. 22, 1913, p. 3.

25. French to Ethel Coe, May 3, 1913, French Papers.

26. One friend living in Paris admonished Hutchinson that Jane Addams's crusade was doing incalculable harm to the Allied cause: "In France to say that one is Pacifist is to say that he is pro-Allemand . . . . *Do do all you can to stop this 'Peace' talk for you only prolong the war.*" Alice Getty to Hutchinson, July 8, 1915, Hutchinson Collection.

"HIS MOST PERMANENT MONUMENT," pp. 78–85.

The title of this section comes from a statement by Robert Harshe. See note 14 below.

1. This expansion anticipated the reorganization of the galleries to accommodate installation of the Palmer and Kimball collections, the development of the Department of Oriental Art, and the gifts of period rooms from Kate Buckingham and the heirs of William Hibbard.

2. Philip Gentner to Hutchinson, Nov. 20 [1914/15], Hutchinson Papers.

3. French to Robert W. de Forest, Apr. 26, 1912, French Papers.

4. Robert B. Harshe to the board of trustees of the Art Institute of Chicago, n.d. (memorandum incorporated in the minutes), minutes, Oct. 6, 1921, Board of Trustees Records, AIC Archives.

5. The bulk of the Art Institute's costume collection (including Frances Hutchinson's gifts) was placed on permanent loan at the Chicago Historical Society in the 1960s. A beaded silk bag (American, c. 1840) that she presented to the museum in 1919 remains a part of the collection of the Department of Textiles (1919.187).

6. These books include *Our Country Home: How We Transformed a Wisconsin Woodland* (A. C. McClurg, 1908) and *Our Country Life* (A. C. McClurg, 1912). They were later republished in a single volume as *Wychwood: The History of an Idea* (Lakeside Press, 1928) with an added section titled "Our Final Aim." In 1932 Frances Hutchinson presented the seventy-three-acre estate to the University of Chicago, together with an endowment to maintain it as a wildlife sanctuary and nature preserve. It served as a research laboratory for the university's Botany Department until 1957, when the property was sold to private buyers as permitted by the terms of the gift. Department of Botany Records, box 1, folder 2, Special Collections Research Center, University of Chicago Library.

7. Frances Hutchinson to Frances Glessner, Nov. 7, 1910, Glessner Journals.

8. "Chicago Young Man Commits Suicide," *Chicago Tribune*, July 7, 1909, p. 5. Hutchinson notes attending the funeral in his diary entry for July 13, 1909, box 1, Hutchinson Collection.

9. George L. Herdle to Hutchinson, Dec. 16, 1921, Hutchinson Papers.

10. George Eggers to Charles H. Burkholder, Oct. 15, 1924, memorial scrapbook, box 2, Hutchinson Personal Papers.

11. R. M. F. [Rose Mary Fischkin], "The Charles L. Hutchinson Bequest," *Bulletin of the Art Institute of Chicago* 19, 9 (Dec. 1925), pp. 102–04. At the same time Frances Hutchinson also loaned a group of antiquities, including *Portrait of Antinous*, a Roman marble from the second century A.D. Some of the paintings were later deaccessioned, and in 1941 the museum purchased at auction *Portrait of a Seated Woman* by Antonis Mor (1941.29) as a gift of Charles L. Hutchinson. Frances did retain some notable paintings not mentioned in her husband's will, but these came to the Art Institute upon her death. They include the two oil panels (transferred to canvas) by the Master of the Antwerp Adoration (1936.126, 1936.127) that Hutchinson had acquired from Durand-Ruel in 1890 and the three small oils by David Teniers the Younger that he bought through Thomas Agnew and Sons in 1886 (1936.123, 1936.124, 1936.125).

12. In 1923 trustee Edward E. Ayer gave securities then worth $50,000 to establish a fund for the purchase of art objects to be marked as memorials to his friend Charles Hutchinson. Ayer's stated object was to "forever express his love, admiration and respect for one of the dearest, broadest and most unselfish men he has ever known, and one to whom the people of Chicago are today under more obligations, too, than to any man in the State." Minutes, Jan. 11, 1923, Board of Trustees Records, AIC Archives.

13. The men also supplemented their private collections, but this is the exception that proves the rule because they bequeathed nearly all these treasured items to the museum after their deaths.

14. Helen Lefkowitz Horowitz, *Culture and the City: Cultural Philanthropy in Chicago from the 1880s to 1917* (University Press of Kentucky, 1976), pp. 52–53.

15. Sometimes this happened quite literally, as when the Art Institute began displaying paintings from its collection in Chicago park buildings. Interestingly, it was in fact French who spearheaded this initiative, showing such generational differences are never so clear cut. Horowitz (note 12), p. 157.

16. Robert Harshe, "Charles Lawrence Hutchinson, 1854–1924," *Bulletin of the Art Institute of Chicago* 18, 9 (Dec. 1924), p. 110.

17. Hutchinson, untitled address delivered to the Chicago Literary Club, c. 1915, Hutchinson Collection.